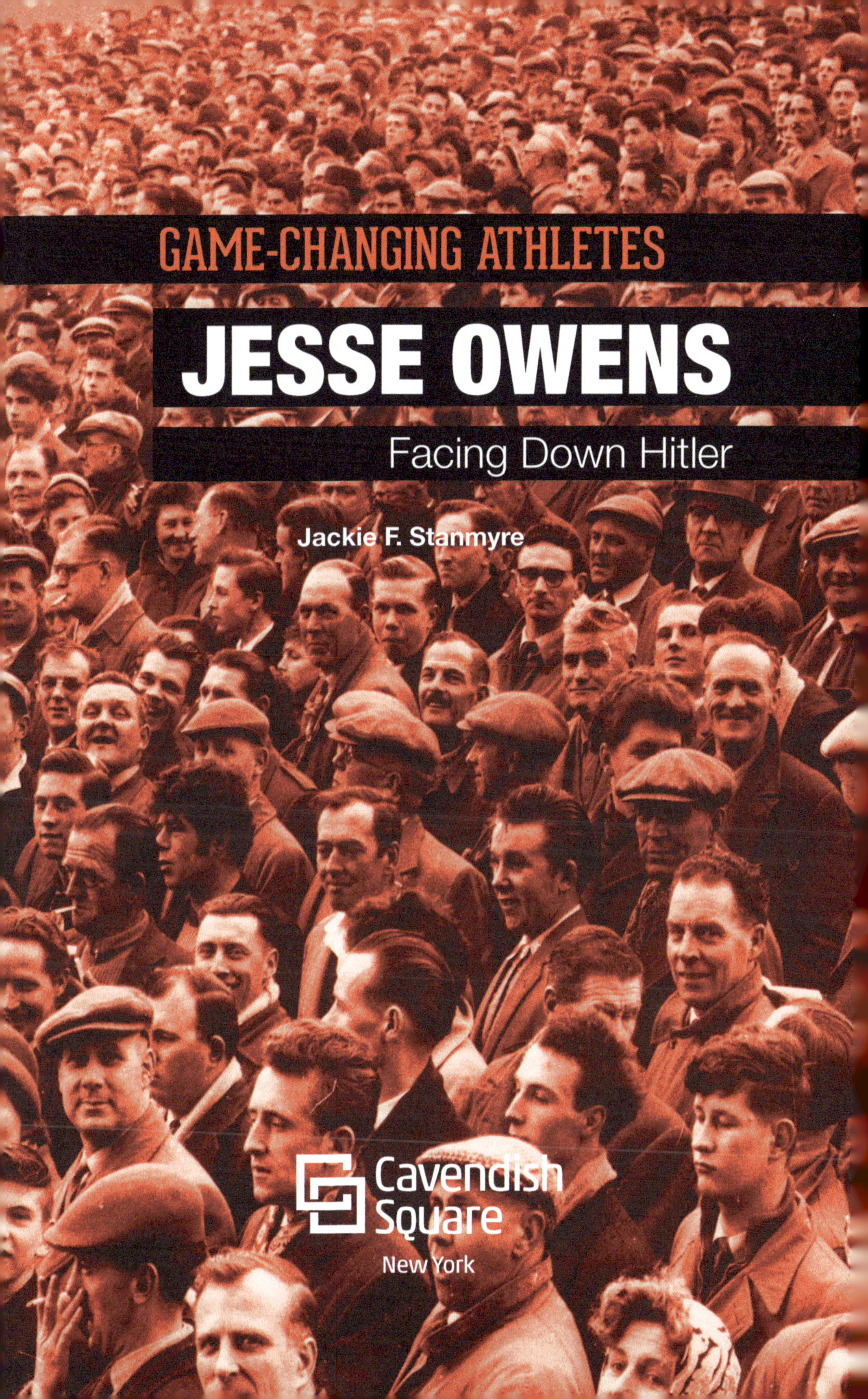

GAME-CHANGING ATHLETES

JESSE OWENS

Facing Down Hitler

Jackie F. Stanmyre

Cavendish Square
New York

Published in 2016 by Cavendish Square Publishing, LLC
243 5th Avenue, Suite 136, New York, NY 10016

First Edition

Website: cavendishsq.com

CPSIA Compliance Information: Batch #CW16CSQ

Cataloging-in-Publication Data

Names: Stanmyre, Jackie F.
Title: Jesse Owens: facing down Hitler / Jackie F. Stanmyre.
Description: New York : Cavendish Square Publishing, 2016 | Series: Game-changing athletes | Includes index.
Identifiers: ISBN 9781502610492 (library bound) | ISBN 9781502610508 (ebook)
Subjects: LCSH: Owens, Jesse, 1913-1980—Juvenile literature. |
Track and field athletes—United States—Biography—Juvenile literature. |
African American track and field athletes—Biography—Juvenile literature.
Classification: LCC GV697.O9 S73 2016 | DDC 796.42'092—dc23

Editorial Director: David McNamara
Editor: Fletcher Doyle
Copy Editor: Rebecca Rohan
Art Director: Jeffrey Talbot
Designer: Joseph Macri
Senior Production Manager: Jennifer Ryder-Talbot
Production Editor: Renni Johnson
Photo Research: J8 Media

The photographs in this book are used by permission and through the courtesy of: Keystone-France/Gamma-Keystone via Getty Images, front, back covers and throughout the book; Getty Images, front cover; Crowd Scene, Norman Potter/Express/Getty Images, throughout the book; Ullstein Bild via Getty Images, 6-7, 11, 43, 59, 70, 73; New York Times Co./Getty Images, 8, 14; AP Photo, 21, 28, 36-37, 62, 82, 84, 91; AP Photo/Paul Cannon, 24; John Vachon for U.S. Farm Security Administration, Library of Congress/File: Segregation 1938.jpg - Wikimedia Commons, 33; Charles Payne/NY Daily News via Getty Images, 46; Fox Photos/Getty Images, 48; Heinrich Hoffmann/Ullstein Bild/Getty Images, 54; Popperfoto/Getty Images, 57; AP Photo/Marty Lederhandler, 67; Austrian Archives/Imagno/Getty Images, 76–77, Günter Peters/Ullstein Bild via Getty Images, 79; Angelo Cozzi/Archivio Mondadori/Getty Images, 88; Art Shay/Sports Illustrated/Getty Images, 93; AP Photo/Richard Drew, 95; JOHN MACDOUGALL/AFP/Getty Images, 98–99.

Printed in the United States of America

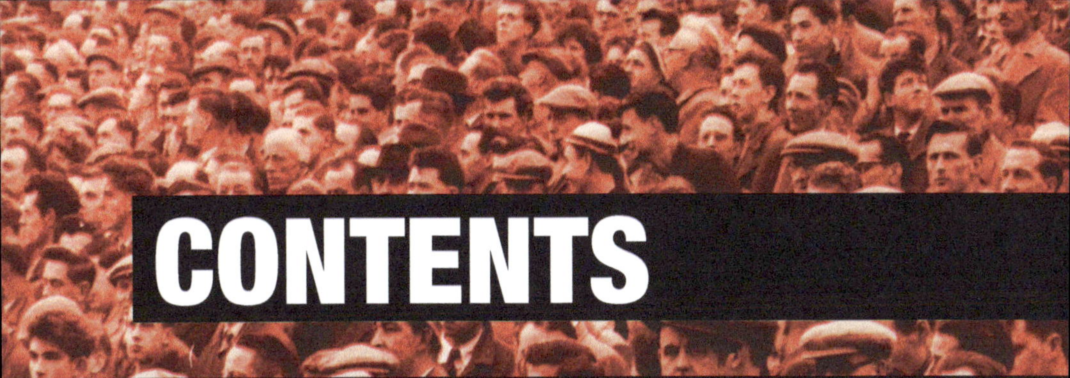

CONTENTS

Introduction 4

Chapter 1: Father's Footsteps 9

Chapter 2: Under a Microscope 29

Chapter 3: Triumph and Controversy 49

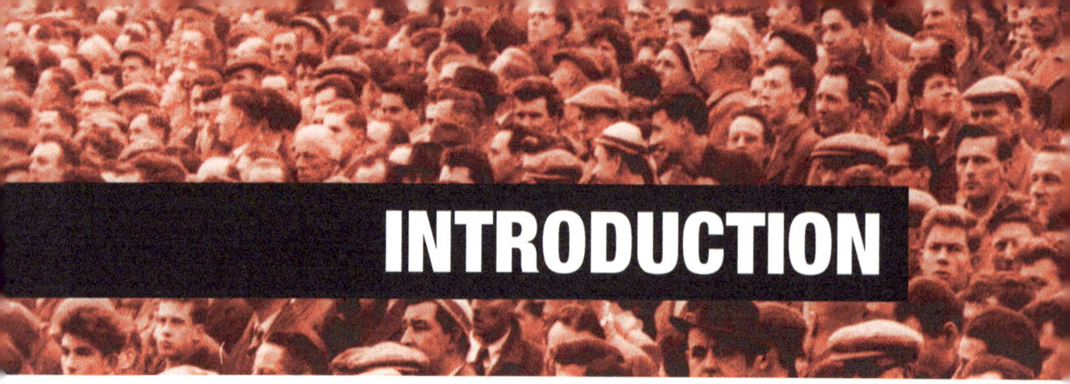

INTRODUCTION

Adolf Hitler had big plans to use the 1936 Berlin Olympics to showcase the superiority of the Aryan race. The German **dictator**, infamous for the future slaughter of millions of Jews and other "undesirables" in the Holocaust, thought he would see blond-haired, fair-skinned, blue-eyed athletes running to victory, proving his point that some groups of people were meant to dominate others. One man proved to the world that this just wasn't so.

Jesse Owens, an African American, was born in Alabama with few resources and even fewer privileges. Upon his family moving to Cleveland, Ohio, Owens began running under the guidance of Charles Riley, who invigorated Owens with different ways to approach his craft: not thinking too much, running lightly on his feet, not straining.

Quickly, it became apparent that Owens possessed a special, never-before-seen talent that would force others to consider their suppositions on racial supremacy. Many battles against **prejudice** and for equal rights were being fought throughout the world—including in America—with violence, through protest, or in courtrooms. Others, like Owens, fought those battles with their natural gifts, saying little with their words but much through their actions.

Owens had made a name for himself in the track-and-field community by excelling at Ohio State University. In 1935, in less than an hour of competition at the Big Ten Championships, Owens had beaten three world records and tied a fourth. Despite the cloud of **discrimination** that hung over the 1936 Games, the long-jumper and sprinter entered into the event with high expectations. And he would meet them all.

Owens left those Olympic Games with four gold medals, earned in the 100-meter and 200-meter (109-yard and 219-yard) dashes, the 4 × 100 **relay**, and the **long jump**. However, he also left the world a bit shaken. A face like Jesse Owens's was to be the picture of athletic excellence? Hitler clearly had been expecting better of "his people." And even some Americans were reluctant to accept Owens as their golden boy. Franklin Delano Roosevelt, the US president at the time, did not even congratulate Owens for his feats.

America and the international community had a long way to go toward the acceptance of members of minority races. On his own two feet, Owens did everything he could to quicken the pace toward equality. He left a legacy, imploring his fellow African Americans—and all Americans—to work toward achieving their dreams and silencing the naysayers.

Jesse Owens was known for his long, easy stride and for showing no signs of strain on his face as he routed the opposition.

779

As a high-school student, Jesse Owens broke the world record in the 100 meters.

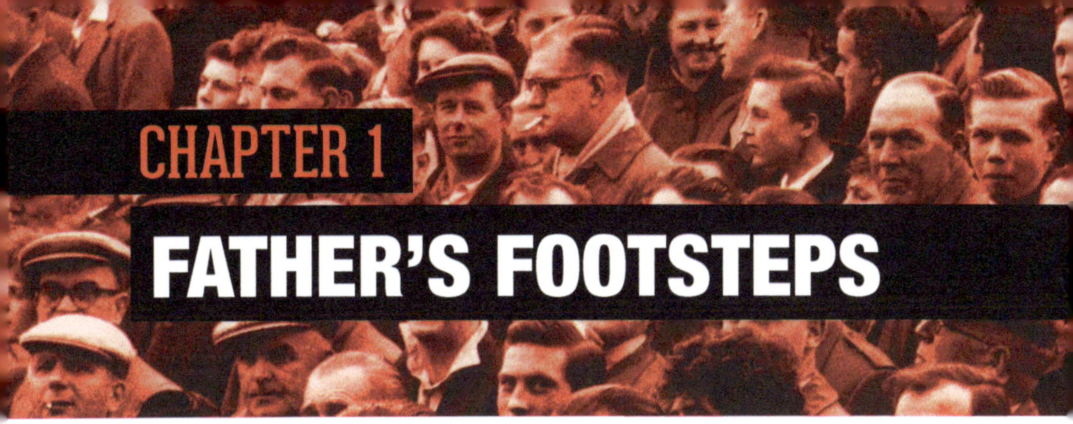

CHAPTER 1

FATHER'S FOOTSTEPS

"Spectators scarcely realized that anyone else was on the field."

—The *Cleveland Gazette* on Jesse Owens

James Cleveland Owens, who came to be known as Jesse, was born September 12, 1913, the youngest of ten children born to Henry Cleveland and Mary Emma (who went by "Emma") Owens in Oakville, Alabama. His parents were sharecroppers, meaning a landowner allowed them to live on 40 acres (16.2 hectares) of land that they were expected to farm and maintain. In exchange for a ramshackle house and use of the farm equipment, the Owens family was to give half the season's crops to the landowner; the other half they could sell to earn money for clothes and basic supplies.

After four a.m. wakeup calls, plowing the fields with a mule, hoeing the rows of corn and cotton, and picking the cotton, little time was available for leisure in the Owens family. But as a young boy, Jesse remembers the pleasure he saw on his father's face whenever he was running. On Sundays after church and before their early bedtime, Henry Owens gathered with men from the surrounding farms and raced across the flatland.

Young Jesse's dreams of racing were born on those Sunday afternoons. "I used to watch [my father] with wide eyes, for he had legs like no other human being I'd ever seen and a way of running that resembled a springing cat," Owens wrote in his autobiography, *The Jesse Owens Story*. "None of the fellows could ever get close to him, but what I loved most was when he'd really let himself out and run away from the others like a locomotive that just blazes past a platform full of people without stopping.

"From the time I went to school, whenever anyone used to ask me who I wanted to be like when I grew up, I'd answer, 'George Washington Carver.' But the truth was that I *really* wanted to be a runner like my father. That's how I thought of him—as a runner—not as a cotton picker. But how could you *run* for a living?"

Owens was best served keeping these ambitions to himself for reasons aside from the curiosity of running for a living. For starters, he was a sickly child who caught pneumonia, which his parents called "the devil's cold," nearly every winter. The family could not afford to pay a doctor, so Owens was wrapped in soft cotton feed sacks and set up in front of the stove for weeks at a time, trying to stave off the illness. He also began developing boils on his chest and legs. His mother played makeshift surgeon, boiling a knife and cutting the bumps off her young son's body. He bled for days. Owens recalled it as his discovery of the true meaning of pain. He credits the fact he survived this experience with his ability to, years later, push through all levels of physical hurt and discomfort when he was training.

By the age of six, Owens was well enough to walk the 9 miles (14.5 kilometers) to school with his brothers and sisters. The teachers were volunteers and rarely highly educated themselves, but they taught Owens to read and write. Still, he wasn't much of a student, as he paid little attention to his lessons and skipped school for extended periods. When harvest season came around, the schools closed to allow the children to assist their families in the fields. Despite the work the Owenses put into their crops, with all they had to turn over to the landowner, little money was left for anything beyond the basics. Ragged clothes were repaired over and over again. The Owens family lived on a diet of mainly beans and onions and drank the same cold water they had to use for showers.

Jesse Owens's parents, Emma (*far left*) and Henry (*far right*), were reluctant to let their son begin running because he was sick as a child. Also pictured is Owens's wife, Ruth.

On a walk home from church one Sunday, the Owens children discussed their dreams. The three daughters said they hoped to marry men with good jobs; one of Jesse's brothers wanted to move to the city and own his own land; Jesse wanted to go to college. Without changing their environment, those dreams would remain unreachable. When tragedy struck a neighbor and friend, Henry Owens came to realize a better life was not in store for his family in Alabama.

The Owens family became part of a large movement of African Americans who left the South for the North in what is known today as the **Great Black Migration**. Approximately 6.5 million African Americans trekked to large urban cities in the North, including Chicago, Buffalo, Detroit, New York City, and Cleveland. Most of those people previously had been farming in the South, with some teaching in schools or preaching in churches. They hoped jobs in industries such as automobile manufacturing would await. As the train prepared to depart, Owens asked his mother where the train would be taking them. She replied: "It's gonna take us to a better life." And she was right.

The new life, though improved, was not easy. Prejudice existed in the North just as it did the South, and many businesses refused to hire African Americans, while many hotels and restaurants refused to serve them. Owens's father had difficulty finding a steady job, which forced his mother to take on work as a cleaning lady. Owens's siblings found odd jobs, working as maids, unloading freight cars, working as part-time janitors. Owens himself had three jobs: pumping gas, caring for flowers at a greenhouse, and shining shoes. Owens would also be the only one lucky enough to stay in school.

In Cleveland, Owens also came to be "Jesse." Until that time he had been called "J.C.," short for James Cleveland. When Owens's teacher asked his name, she misunderstood the boy's response and wrote his name down as "Jesse." Afraid to interrupt his teacher on the first day of school, J.C. became Jesse and would remain that way.

Shortly after moving to Cleveland and getting adjusted to his work schedule and school schedule, Owens would meet a man who would forever change his life. Charles Riley, the athletics coach of the grammar and high schools and Owens's gym teacher, asked the young boy to come out for the track team. Owens's mother was reluctant to let him participate, for fear of him getting hurt. The young boy had spent such a large portion of his life being sick and skinny, she was afraid for him to try anything too strenuous.

Owens worked on convincing his father, saying, "I want to grow up to be strong, and be a runner like you were," he recalled in *The Jesse Owens Story*. The following morning, he woke up to find his father had convinced his mother to let him give it a try. The next order of business would be arranging a training schedule. Riley encouraged Owens to come after school, but that was when the boy was heading off to one of his three jobs. They came to an agreement to meet at the track forty-five minutes before

At Ohio State, Jesse Owens's difficulties would be in the classroom—not on the track.

the school day began. By the time Owens entered junior high, he was one of the fastest runners in his class.

In eighth grade, though, Owens hit a wall. He ran quarter-mile (0.4 km) races against much older boys and he rarely won. He was disheartened but not discouraged. He threw question after question at Riley about what he could do to win. The answer came with a Sunday drive; Riley told Owens they were going to watch the best runners in the whole world. After hours in the car, Riley turned in to a horse racetrack, where he instructed Owens to watch the winning horses' expressions and movements.

Owens recalled the horses moving as if they weren't trying, their faces blank and void of emotion. "Do you know why the best horses make it look easy? Because the determination is all on the inside where no one can see it," Riley told Owens, he recalled in *The Legend of Jesse Owens*. Owens took that lesson to heart. He learned to mimic the horses and their easy, fluid, and powerful movements. Riley taught the boys on his team to run as lightly as possible, their feet barely touching the ground. He taught them to look straight ahead to the finish line and not concentrate on the other runners. No energy was to be wasted.

Riley apparently knew early on that Owens's strength would be in the short sprints, but Owens trained for and ran in much longer races in order to build his endurance. Owens grew to understand the demands of each distance, as well. During one attempt at the 220-yard (201 m) dash, he approached it with the all-out effort he was known to give in the 100-yard (91 m) dash. He ultimately crossed the finish line third, after being passed at the end. Owens kept running until he came to a brick wall, which he hit hard. He bruised his elbow and was gasping in pain when Riley approached him, Owens recalled in *The Legend of Jesse Owens*. "Congratulations, Jesse," Riley said. "You won today. Even when the race was over, you didn't stop." Riley meant it. In addition to his speed and strength, Owens was building character.

When Owens was twelve, his mother came to watch him race. He won by a large margin, and Riley then pulled Emma Owens aside and told her, "Mrs. Owens, your son has the most unusual pair of twelve-year-old legs on earth. I know this will shock you, but Jesse could become an Olympic champion," Owens recalled in *The Jesse Owens Story*. But Riley never let this be known to Owens himself. He downplayed how fast the boy was running, often telling him there was much more work to be done. He shrugged when Owens asked for his times, giving approximations that were less impressive. "Don't worry about running fast," Riley said. "Just run *right*."

On one occasion, Riley timed Owens running 100 yards—then measured to assure the distance wasn't an inch short. Showing Owens the stopwatch that read eleven seconds flat, Riley beamed. "My boy," he said, "You have tied the [schoolboy] world record." Owens would also set junior high school records with a 6-foot (1.82 meters) high jump and a long jump of 22 feet, 11¾ inches (7 m).

Around this time, Riley introduced Owens to an inspirational figure who would ignite Owens's dream of going to the Olympics. Track star Charley Paddock visited Cleveland on a lecture tour in 1928. Paddock had won two gold medals (100 meters and 4 × 100-meter relay) and one silver (200 meters) at the 1920 Olympics in Antwerp, Belgium, and earned silver (200 meters) in the 1924 Olympics in Paris. After speaking to students at Fairmount Junior High, Paddock met with Owens in Riley's office, where he told the young runner about competing in races around the world. This may have been the first time Owens truly learned about the Olympics. From that point forward, he dreamed of making the US Olympic team.

In 1930, Owens entered East Technical High School, a trade school that would neither challenge him academically nor teach him the study skills needed for college. Most of his classmates were preparing for jobs, not college. The change in schools also temporarily led to a separation from Riley. To Owens's benefit, his new coach, Edgar Weil, recognized he was not equipped to coach an athlete of Owens's caliber. His expertise was in football. He brought on Riley, who was in his fifties and had decades of experience, as an assistant coach.

Owens was seventeen when he started high school, and he faced two situations that threatened his athletic pursuits. First, his father was hit by a taxicab and suffered a broken leg that forced him out of work. Then Owens's brothers were laid off from the steel mill and moved their

LIFE WITH RILEY

Charles Riley grew up in Mauch Chunk, Pennsylvania, and attended Temple University in Philadelphia. After graduation, he was offered the job as teacher and coach at Fairmount Junior High School, where he would coach Jesse Owens. Riley also served as a secondary father figure to Owens. Despite the informal and legal **segregation** of the era, Riley, who was white, invited Owens into his home and treated him as a member of the family.

Owens said of Riley: “He was the first white man I really knew, and without even trying, he proved to me beyond all proof that a white man can understand—and love—a Negro,” according to *Jesse Owens: An American Life*.

Owens trusted Riley immensely, hanging on every word of advice he had to offer. He learned the running and jumping form that would propel him to Olympic glory, and he developed the confidence to overcome the racial barriers thrust upon a young African-American athlete of his generation.

Riley’s commitment to Owens was apparent, as the two held early-morning practices so Owens could work after school. Owens was quoted in *Jesse Owens: Champion Athlete* as having said: “Every morning, just like in Alabama, I got up with the sun, ate my breakfast even before my mother and sisters and brothers, and went to school, winter, spring, and fall alike to run and jump and bend my body this way and that for Mr. Charles Riley.” On Owens’s commitment, Riley said: “He was a boy who yearned for every bit of instruction I could give him, and he was always the last to quit practice,” according to *The Guardian*.

In discussing the 1936 Olympics with *The Guardian*, Owens said of Riley's influence: "It was the final of the 100 meters that was the most nerve-wracking. You see, you come through months of training and you come now to the point where you have six men in the final and these six men represent the fastest human beings in the world. Now you begin to realize that out of it is going to come only one winner. He is everything—nobody else matters. The loser, and there are five of them, is just another fellow.

"The gun goes off and you run this race according to the way you've planned it in your mind—evenly and in front. And I was in front and then I had a lapse of memory. I forgot what I was trying to do and I thought instead in terms of an Olympic record. But records are not made that way, I tightened up and out of the corner of my eye I could feel the field coming up and then just like a flash it all came back. Charles Riley's words: relax, relax. And the arms begin to move freely again and it's all looseness and you **hit the tape** and then all the jubilation and all the pressures and everything is gone."

Sadly, during Riley's later years he lost contact with his former pupil. He saw Owens for the first time in almost fifteen years when the athlete was honored at a 1960 television broadcast of *This Is Your Life*. That would also be the last meeting, as Riley died later that year.

wives and children into their parents' already-crowded home. Emma Owens convinced her youngest son to stay in school despite the family's desperate need for financial support. None of his siblings would finish high school.

To help at home, Owens obtained a job delivering groceries 2 miles (3.2 km) from home, which gave him an excuse for an extra two-mile run each day.

At the track meets, fans came to see not *if* Owens would win, but by how much he would win. Then, with his athletic stock on the rise, Owens's personal life would cause turmoil from another angle. His girlfriend, Ruth, was pregnant. She quit school and focused her attention on earning money by working at a beauty parlor. Owens's biography stated the two eloped to Erie, Pennsylvania, where a justice of the peace performed their wedding ceremony. However, no marriage certificate exists from this time, leading many to believe the wedding did not actually take place and that Jesse and Ruth claimed it had to prevent their daughter from the stigma of being an illegitimate child. Owens recalls their wedding dinner was hot dogs and orange drink, and their marriage was meant to be a secret, as neither of their parents supported it.

Later, during an argument with Ruth's father about the amount of time Owens was spending at their home, Owens blurted out that the two had been married. Accounts vary as to Ruth's parents' response; Owens at times claimed the two were forced to move in together, while at other times he stated he was restricted from seeing Ruth. As

Jesse Owens (*center*) and his high school sweetheart, Minnie Ruth Solomon, publicly exchanged marriage vows on July 5, 1935.

if the increased pressures of preparing for a child weren't enough added pressure for the young star, Owens received distressing news: the city barred married students from participating in sports. While the devastation was real, it also was short-lived. Riley came to his rescue, convincing the school board to change its rule. Owens would be able to compete.

This all was occurring behind the scenes as Owens trained for the **Olympic trials**. He headed to the Northwestern University campus in Evanston, Illinois, to try out for the Olympic team. With the 1932 Olympics to be held in Los Angeles, more attention than ever was placed on the trials—and the African-American community had expectations of seeing many black athletes among the competitors. Owens would be running against college-level athletes who far surpassed the competition he had faced in Cleveland. A nervous Owens lost his concentration.

He competed in the 100-yard and 220-yard dashes and the long jump. Owens was outdone by Ralph Metcalfe, who was then attending Marquette University in Milwaukee, Wisconsin, and Eddie Tolan from the University of Michigan. That summer marked the beginning of a long friendship and rivalry between Owens and Metcalfe. After one of the losses to Metcalfe that summer, a still-winded Owens extended his hand to Metcalfe and said, "I thought I had you," he recalled in *The Legend of Jesse Owens*. "Maybe that's what beat you, Jesse," Metcalfe responded. A student of the sport, Owens learned a lesson: no previous successes guaranteed victory in the present or in the future. The thought intensified his training.

As Owens would later learn, he didn't lose just to the fastest Americans. Tolan and Metcalfe finished first and second in the 100-meter dash and first and third in the 200-meter (240-yard) race during the Olympics themselves. Owens could compete with world-level talent and would continue to prove that in the coming months. After the Olympics, some of the runners toured the United States, holding demonstration track meets. This time, Owens was ready. He won the 100-yard and 220-yard dashes and finished second in the long jump behind the 1932 Olympic gold medalist, Edward Gordon, when the squad came through Cleveland.

On August 8, 1932, Ruth gave birth to Owens's daughter, Gloria Shirley. Most accounts state that Ruth's parents refused to allow Owens to be fully involved in the child's or their daughter's life, which opened up Owens's schedule so he could focus on running. Entering his senior year of high school, Owens was voted student body president by his classmates (his class was 95 percent white), as well as captain of the track team. The magnetic runner had attracted a passionate following that traveled to meets, cheering him on everywhere he went.

Owens finished his high school career on top. In the spring of 1933, at the Ohio state high school meet, he broke the national high school long-jump record by 3 inches, with a leap of 24 feet, 3¾ inches (7.4 m). In June, at the National Interscholastic Championships in Chicago, he would best

Jesse Owens (*left*) and Ralph Metcalfe were two of the preeminent American sprinters of the 1930s.

his own record in the long jump, flying 24 feet, 9⅗ inches (7.6 m). At the same meet, he set a world record of 20.7 seconds in the 220-yard dash and tied a world record of 9.4 seconds in the 100-yard dash. Owens's high school, East Tech, easily won the meet as Owens himself scored thirty of the team's fifty-four points. In track and field, team points are awarded to the top individual finishers, with winners receiving the highest total.

Owens and his teammates were greeted back in Cleveland with a victory parade. Owens and his parents sat in the backseat of a convertible on the slow-moving procession through the city's downtown, and Charles Riley sat in the car directly behind theirs. The procession stopped in front of City Hall, where the mayor of Cleveland praised the young athlete.

His college search had begun months earlier, as schools across the country heard of the records Owens was breaking. Some days, he would receive letters from three or four colleges at a time, all looking for the track star to join their squads. Colleges in the East and Midwest had **integrated** before the turn of the twentieth century, and African Americans had distinguished themselves on the athletic fields and in the classrooms. However, colleges below the Mason-Dixon line remained segregated for decades after Owens finished high school. At that time, there were no colleges offering athletic scholarships. Instead, students of high athletic caliber were offered easy jobs at good wages to help them offset the costs of tuition. Of course, that didn't stop some schools from offering Owens more behind closed doors: one school promised free room and board and a job for $150 a week. However, Owens wasn't interested in keeping secrets. "You've got to keep running, Jesse, but not dishonestly," Riley told Owens, he recalled in *The Jesse Owens Story*.

He seriously considered the University of Michigan, which is where Riley was encouraging him to go, but ultimately, Owens chose to stay in his home state and attend Ohio State University in Columbus. Many in the African-American community questioned this decision, as Ohio State had a history of poor race relations. The school previously had refused to allow two African-American students to share campus housing with white women; this decision was upheld by Ohio's Supreme Court. One black newspaper accused him of advertising "an institution that majors in prejudice," according to *The Legend of Jesse Owens*. But Owens would not be swayed. He pointed to his own track record: he had become arguably the most popular student in a predominantly white high school already and saw no reason he could not continue this trend in college.

The financial hurdle was easily overcome, as Owens was offered a job running an elevator at the State House. The next step would be the academics: Owens had slipped through high school with a D average, which was not up to the standards of the Ohio State administration. The school allowed him to take several examinations to bypass the normal requirements. Under present-day regulations from the National Collegiate Athletic Association (NCAA), these allowances almost certainly would not have been possible. But at the time, the school lowered its standards to admit this superior athlete. He was one of approximately one hundred African Americans to attend Ohio State University in 1933.

Despite his athletic prowess and the status he could bring to his college, Owens experienced the discrimination others had warned about. As an African American, he was not allowed to live in the male dormitory. He lived instead in a boarding house in the African-American section of Columbus. He had to cook his own meals, as many local restaurants served whites only. Owens's job also had been selected based on his skin color: He operated a freight elevator, as only white athletes were allowed to operate passenger elevators. Life on the track, fortunately, came as easy as ever.

Larry Snyder (*right*) coached Jesse Owens at Ohio State and helped him set high goals in the long jump.

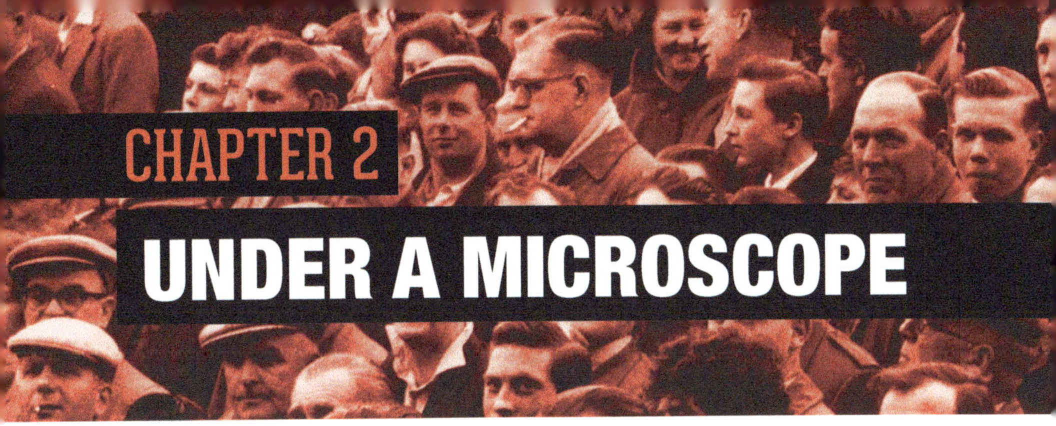

CHAPTER 2

UNDER A MICROSCOPE

"I broke out that Saturday in Michigan. It wasn't only overcoming physical pain; it had to do with overcoming something psychological inside myself."

—Jesse Owens, on May 25, 1935, according to *Triumph*

College freshmen were not allowed to participate on varsity teams, but they could take part in intense training sessions. Owens's new coach, Larry Snyder, had him focus on the motions of his hands and arms to propel himself forward that much more quickly. Snyder also experimented with different **stances** at the starting line, settling on one that required Owens's feet to be closer together, allowing him to react faster to the starting gun. Owens recalled in *The Jesse Owens Story* the many intricacies of Snyder's coaching tactics, including how to direct all his movements forward, ways to stop bobbing when he ran, how not to strain, and how not to overstride. By the time he could compete in varsity meets, Owens's arms would be synchronized with his legs, and he had learned to watch the eyes of the starter, to enhance his ability to come off the starting line as fast as possible.

Snyder also had expertise in the long jump, where he had high expectations for his star pupil as he crept close to an unthinkable 26-foot (7.9 m) leap. Snyder taught

Owens to run through the air, pumping his arms and legs for more distance while he was airborne.

Snyder told *Scholastic Coach* magazine that Owens was extremely open to suggestion. "I have coached a few boys who were very, very good, but who were not easy to coach," Snyder said. "They thought they knew how to do things, and did not want to change, and the work had to be done in a roundabout manner with them; then when the idea came to them as their idea, it was good. [In contrast,] Jesse Owens listens and then he tries to put the suggestions into practice. He is so well coordinated that even a radical 'form' change in starting, or any other part of running, becomes a part of his style after a very few practice sessions."

In addition to being coachable, Owens also was a team player. He added the low hurdles and the mile relay to his list of events, and he took his training for them seriously, as well.

His freshman year, Owens was allowed to participate in **exhibition** meets. He was awarded a spot on the **Amateur Athletic Union** (AAU) All-American team and given the opportunity to compete in the national championship meet in New York. He finished in second, right behind Ralph Metcalfe. Owens also competed in an exhibition at which the judges allowed him to take a running start, more for fun than anything. He finished the race in 8.4 seconds. At the **Big Ten Conference meet** at Ohio State, Owens competed against the other freshman athletes and established records in the 100- and 220-yard dashes and the long jump.

The more difficult part of Owens's first year in college came in the classroom. As the country remained in the Great Depression, Ohio State had cut back on its faculty, meaning a higher student-to-teacher ratio. Owens did not get the individual attention he needed, and, unlike today, there were no academic advisors or tutors assigned to work with the athletes. The only luxury he had was the assistance of coaches who helped him sign up for easier courses. He enrolled in the physical education department and still received poor grades. The greatest academic success came in a class in phonetics, in which Owens overcame his lifelong stuttering problem and learned to speak well.

While balancing athletics and academics, Owens worked the equivalent of a full-time job, between his time operating the elevator, waiting tables in a dining hall (that provided him with free meals), and performing various duties in the school library. As he ran the freight elevator at night, when traffic was extremely slow, he was able to do much of his studying. However, he continued to suffer, never having had proper instruction on how to study and needing more attention than his professors could provide. By his sophomore year, he was on academic probation, making him at risk for failing out of Ohio State altogether.

His sophomore year, Owens learned he would be treated differently than his white teammates. The white varsity athletes would travel together in nice cars, while the African-American athletes rode in clunkers. He recalled feeling disturbed that his white teammates had no problem eating in restaurants from which he and his black teammates had been denied service.

Around this time, Owens determined he would be more a peacemaker than a rabble-rouser when it came to racial matters. He followed in line with Booker T. Washington's mantra that African Americans could work toward progress through education and entrepreneurship, not by fighting. On one particular occasion, Owens's stance would be put to the test. During a road trip, his white teammates brought him and his African-American teammates food from a "white only" restaurant to eat in their car. The restaurant owner snatched the plates from the athletes' hands, with food flying everywhere, staining their clothes and the interior of the car. Not only did Owens keep his cool, he prevented his African-American teammates from retaliating as well.

Owens knew his athletic success put him not only in the spotlight but also under a microscope, and plenty of naysayers would be ready to judge one wrong move, claiming his actions as a representation of his whole race. He even grew frustrated when the media constantly made reference to his skin color, nicknaming him the "Dark Streak," "Tan Thunderbolt," and "Brown Bombshell." Still, he remained polite. He signed autographs for everyone while wondering if they harbored racist thoughts.

"[Racism] can be pure as hell at times and can shake anyone's sureness," he said in *The Legend of Jesse Owens*. "Often it's worse if you were the world's fastest human.

While segregation of blacks and whites was a sign of the times, Jesse Owens worked to keep his cool regarding racial matters.

When you walk into [a fine establishment] wearing a face almost everyone recognizes and still feel that agonizing fear reflex deep in your gut, you still can't help wondering with a part of your soul whether the maître d's smile is a sneer and if the woman at the next table thinks you should be waiting on her instead of sitting next to her. It's worse than if you were simply an anonymous black man." Getting noticed was the price of success, and Owens's stock was soaring.

A few days before he solidified his legend in the Big Ten Championships, Owens made a foolish decision to play football with his friends. He recalled receiving the football with the score tied as he eluded all the defenders on the way to the end zone. Then came the celebration; as his teammates piled on and Owens sought to carry them toward the other goal line, pain slashed through his back. (Differing accounts say Owens injured his back falling down the stairs after roughhousing with fraternity brothers.) He conferred with Snyder, who encouraged

Owens to stay off his feet until meet day, but the pain still would not subside. Snyder said he should sit out the meet so as not to ruin any future opportunities—or Olympic dreams. Owens pled with his coach to compete; he ultimately convinced Snyder to allow him to test out his back in the 100-yard dash.

That decision led to the greatest one-day performance in track and field history, on May 25, 1935, at the Big Ten Championships in Ann Arbor, Michigan. At 3:15 p.m., in the 100-yard dash, the pain was forgotten once the starting gun sounded and Owens crossed the finish line in 9.4 seconds, as fast as any man in the world had ever run before.

He said he wanted to give the long jump a try, too. Owens even placed a towel next to the **pit** at 26 feet, 2 inches (7.98 m)—the then world record. At 3:25 p.m., hanging in the air, he saw his body surpass the towel. With instant thoughts of doubt—did he put the towel in the right place? Did the wind blow the towel?—Owens awaited the measurement. He had broken the world record by more than half a foot (.15 m), with a mark of 26 feet, 8¼ inches (8.13 m). The record would hold for twenty-five years.

At 3:34 p.m., in the 220-yard dash, Owens shaved four-tenths of a second off his previous best time and reclaimed the world record. Owens recalls in *The Jesse Owens Story* that Ralph Metcalfe approached him at this time and said, "There're no more worlds left for you to conquer today, Jess."

But Metcalfe was wrong. Owens was signed up to run the 220-yard low hurdles, his worst event, which came only two races after the 220-yard dash. He told his coach he wanted in. At exactly 4 p.m., Owens positioned himself in the **starting blocks** and ripped away from the competition. He crossed the finish line first and awaited his time. A minute later it was announced: 22.6 seconds, the fastest time in world history.

In less than an hour, Jesse Owens had broken three world records and tied a fourth.

Riley was among the twelve thousand in the stands that day and likely wasn't the only one who shed a tear at the unbelievable success that befell the young star. As he saw Owens getting mobbed by autograph-seekers and reporters, he swung his Model T around the back of the locker room. After showering and getting dressed, Owens snuck out a back window and hopped in the car alongside his coach. The two drove through the night back to Cleveland, talking about all the ways in which Owens's life would never again be the same.

Snyder, his Ohio State coach, spoke with Owens about translating his athletic fame into being a role model for appropriate social behavior, wholesome attitudes, and good interracial relations. "He was constantly on me about the job that I was to do and the responsibility that I had upon the campus. And how I must be able to carry myself because people were looking," Owens recalled in *Jesse Owens: An American Life*. "Everybody's eyes were upon you. And they

On May 25, 1935, Jesse Owens broke three world records and tied a fourth at the Big Ten Championships.

OHIO

would scrutinize everything that you did and so you had to be very careful of the things that you did."

Owens could have been more careful. Within a couple of weeks of his glorious day, Owens met Los Angeles socialite Quincella Nickerson. The two took to dancing and dining together while Owens was competing on the West Coast. With the spotlight intensified, the camera flashes burst brighter, too. Pictures of Owens and Nickerson showed up in the local papers with hints of a wedding engagement. It appeared at this time that Owens and Ruth were not officially married—but still had a long-term relationship as well as a child together. And Ruth wasn't happy. She caught up with him by phone, and one can only guess at the words that were exchanged. The message clearly shook Owens, who, after winning ten events in a row, lost all his races at the AAU Championships to Eulace Peacock. The next day, he took the first train back to Cleveland and married Ruth. Still rattled, Owens finished the season losing to Peacock in his final three meets. The *Los Angeles Times* wrote of Peacock: "Swing wide the gates for a new sports hero." Charley Paddock, the former Olympian and Owens's childhood idol, said Owens seemed "pretty well burned out."

With doubt in the air, Owens headed back to Cleveland for his job pumping gas on the night shift. Controversy continued stirring. After his freshman year, Owens had left his job working on the freight elevator and taken a job as a page in the Ohio house of representatives, with his sister's help. The arrangement allowed for Owens to continue receiving pay throughout the summer months, despite the fact he was on the road competing through June and July. This looked to the AAU as if Owens was receiving money without doing the required job. The consequences of breaking the "amateur" code included suspension and athletic ineligibility.

Owens appeared before the committee in mid-August and confirmed that he had received $159 between June 9 and July 31 without having been in Columbus to work. He also stated that he had informed his coaches of the job proposition, and they had advised him to accept it. Ultimately, Owens offered to return the money, and the AAU found he should be allowed to compete. One AAU spokesman concluded, "Knowing the facts as we do, we have considered Owens to be a victim of circumstances and offended, rather than offending any of the provisions of the AAU." The hurdles Owens would face did not end with the politics. He was suspended from the track team for the winter season for his poor grades. He trained on his own, continuing to work toward his goal of competing in the 1936 Olympics.

America's participation in those Olympics wasn't even ensured. In 1932, the International Olympic Committee decided the Games would be held in Germany. Since taking power in 1933, the Nazi Party began preparing for the opportunity to showcase the success of the economic and social policies that guided their government. Adolf Hitler, the autocratic German chancellor, also saw the Olympics as a chance to prove his theories about the superiority of

SCORECARD

High School: Set national records in the 100-yard dash, 220-yard dash, and long jump.

College: 1935: NCAA titles in 100-yard dash, 220-yard dash, 200-meter low hurdles, and long jump; 1936: NCAA titles in 100-yard dash, 220-yard dash, 220-yard low hurdles, and long jump.

Amateur Athletic Union: Six titles, five in the long jump.

1936 Summer Olympics:
Gold Medal in 100-meter dash
Gold Medal and World Record in 200-meter dash
Gold Medal and World Record in 4 × 100-meter relay
Gold Medal and World Record in long jump

Awards and Honors: Alabama Sports Hall of Fame inductee, 1970; USA Track and Field Hall of Fame, 1974; Presidential Medal of Freedom recipient, 1976; USA Track and Field creates the Jesse Owens Award, honoring the country's top track and field athlete annually, 1981; US Olympic Hall of Fame inductee, 1983; a street near the Olympic Stadium in Berlin was renamed Jesse-Owens-Allee, 1984; Congressional Gold Medal recipient, posthumously, 1990; Owens's hometown dedicates Jesse Owens Memorial Park and Museum, 1996; Ohio State University dedicates Jesse Owens Memorial Stadium, 2001.

"Aryan" people, meaning those with fair skin, light-colored eyes, and light hair. Excluded from the supposed "master race" were Jewish people, gypsies, and blacks, among others. Jews were banned from Germany's amateur sports clubs, members of which were the only ones who could try out for the Olympic team.

While Germany had a small black minority, Hitler and the Nazi Party's stance on them was explicitly clear. "Negroes have no place at an Olympiad," wrote one German writer, according to *The Legend of Jesse Owens.* "The ancient Greeks would turn in their graves if they knew what modern men have made out of their holy … Games. The blacks must be excluded. We expect nothing less."

In order to maintain Germany's role as host country, Hitler was forced to cave in to the demands of the International Olympic Committee, allowing for a full representation of all races and religions at the Olympics. He did this begrudgingly, as Nazi scientists sought to invalidate Owens's—and other black athletes'—status as human beings. Some presented scientific "findings" that Owens would have been able to run so well because of bone conformation and animal-like muscular energy. Years later, Jesse said, "There is no difference between the races. If the black athlete has been better than his white counterpart, it's because he's hungrier—he wants it more," according to *The Legend of Jesse Owens.*

So, Germany would let him in, but would America want to send him? The president of the AAU, Judge Jeremiah

T. Murphy, heard of the persecution of the Jews in Nazi Germany and called for a boycott of the games. Former Olympian Avery Brundage, the president of the American Olympic Association, initially supported a boycott, on the grounds that Jewish Germans were being barred from competition. In order to form a more educated opinion, Brundage visited Germany. He was given tours of facilities and met with Jewish leaders, though always under the accompaniment of Nazis. He saw what Hitler wanted him to see, which, at the time, was enough to convince him that a boycott was unnecessary. After Brundage's visit, however, the debate would reignite. Hitler issued the Nuremberg Laws in September 1935, depriving German Jews of equal protection under the law. (Not all Americans believed discriminatory practices were in place: Frederick W. Rubien, the secretary of the American Olympic Association, famously said, "Germans are not discriminating against Jews in their Olympic trials. The Jews are eliminated because they are not good enough as athletes.")

The African-American press in the United States took on its own stance. How could a group of Americans be so concerned about discriminatory practices abroad when such practices were still taking place in their own backyard? African Americans still were absent from major league baseball and football teams and most universities' athletic teams. Editors of African-American publications seemed split: Some supported the boycott, in favor of protesting racism "in its every manifestation," according to *Jesse*

Avery Brundage (*left*) was instrumental in deciding that Americans would compete in the Berlin Olympics. He's shown here in 1936 with Ritter von Halt, president of the German National Olympic Committee.

Owens: An American Life. Others, however, thought success of African-American athletes at an event as prominent as the Olympics would open the eyes of not only the Nazi Germans but also the white Americans at home who still had their doubts about the abilities of blacks.

The circumstances put Owens in a unique position. Of course he didn't support discrimination, but this was his Olympic dream. In a November 1935 interview, Owens publicly announced, "If there is discrimination against minorities in Germany, then we must withdraw from the Olympics." Quickly, Snyder asked him to reconsider his stance. Discrimination against African-American athletes was routine in the South. Northern schools were asked to leave their black athletes at home as a condition for playing in some college football bowl games. The Sugar Bowl track meet being held in New Orleans that same fall had not invited Owens and other African-American athletes. Snyder pointed out that no one was suggesting *that meet* be canceled due to the exclusion. "Why should we oppose Germany for doing something that we do right here at home?" Snyder asked, according to *Jesse Owens: An American Life*. Owens did not speak publicly on the matter again, but others joined the discussion. African-American newspapers and leaders in the community pled with him to stand his ground. He received a telegram from Walter White, the secretary of the National Association for the Advancement of Colored People (NAACP) stating: "Participation by American athletes, and especially those of our own race, which has suffered more than any other from American race hatred, would, I firmly believe, do irreparable harm. If the Hitlers and Mussolinis of the world are successful it is inevitable that dictatorships based upon prejudice will spread throughout the world, as indeed they are now spreading."

White felt Owens could strike a blow at intolerance by sacrificing his Olympic dream. Owens considered White among the most respected men in the African-American community. But he felt ill equipped to take on this political battle. He knew, however, that he had worked his whole life to achieve Olympic glory. Without even needing to consult with Snyder, Owens decided if Americans would be going to Berlin, he wanted to be one of them. On December 8, 1935, the AAU decided American athletes would compete in Germany.

Meanwhile, Owens's grades continued to keep him away from the track. A few days after Christmas that year, he received word that he had failed a psychology course and would remain ineligible for the winter indoor track season. Still, Owens traveled with the team, and his resolve was tested. He and his African-American teammates continued to face discrimination on the road, as they were refused admission to a restaurant in Richmond, Indiana, and later Indianapolis. Owens advocated for backing down when his teammates wanted to fight.

During one "open" meet that winter, in which Owens was allowed to compete, he raced alongside Eulace Peacock. In the 50-yard (46 m) dash, Peacock's starting blocks slipped and Owens ran to easy victory. When Owens saw what had happened, he insisted the race be rerun. He finished that second race a few inches behind Peacock, leading to more questions about whether Owens was ready for real competition. He had a lot to prove: of his six major races from July 4, 1935 through April 1936, he had lost all but one to Peacock.

The downfall of Peacock was swift and unfortunate. Less than four months before the Games' opening ceremony, and in Owens's first important meet in almost a full calendar year, Peacock snapped his hamstring. The battle of the Goliaths between Owens and Peacock that everyone was prepared to watch never came to fruition. Peacock would not recover in time for the Olympics, perhaps rerouting the path of history.

Eulace Peacock (*Temple*) was regularly beating Jesse Owens (*Ohio*) before Peacock snapped his hamstring prior to the Olympics, perhaps rewriting history.

Meanwhile, Owens's star was on the rise. In five successive meets between Ohio State and other Big Ten schools, Owens would break world, conference, or local meet records. At the Big Ten finals, he won all four of his events for the second consecutive year and set records in two of them. His idle winter spent away from competition had fueled Owens's determination. Owens easily qualified at the regional Olympic trials in Chicago that June and ultimately finished first in the finals in the 100- and 200-meter sprints and in the long jump.

Owens was one of nineteen African-American athletes—twelve in track and field (two of whom were women), five in boxing, and two in weightlifting—who would represent the United States in Berlin. The trend was moving toward African-American inclusion—and success. In 1924, three African Americans earned Olympic medals. In 1932, four African Americans on the team brought home five medals among them. The *Los Angeles Times* even issued a warning with their headline: "Colored Boys Sports Threat: Athletic Prominence Grows Year after Year."

Around the same time, Elmer A. Carter wrote in *Opportunity*, according to *Jump for Joy*: "That the Negro was deficient in the qualities of which athletic champions are made was long one of the accepted shibboleths of the American people. That rare combination—stamina, skill, and courage—it was commonly believed were seldom found under a black skin. Like many other myths concerning the Negro, this myth is being exploded not by theory, nor argument, but by performance."

With the 1936 Olympics on the horizon and names like Owens and boxer Joe Louis headlining the American team, the editor of the *Call and Post*, an African-American newspaper, wrote of the excitement this created for the next generation. "The Negro youth has been starved for their own heroes a mighty long time. Everything they have seen glorified in the past has been white. They have heard of Babe Ruth, Jack Dempsey, etc. But deep down in their little hearts, they have gone to bed and reflected that, after all, these fellows are white. A hero of their own flesh and blood, they have lacked." Until now.

Adolf Hitler hoped the Olympics would showcase Aryan strength.

CHAPTER 3

TRIUMPH AND CONTROVERSY

"I was getting ready for a battle with a madman who would try to rule the entire world."

—Jesse Owens in *The Jesse Owens Story*

The events in Germany in the 1930s appear more in history books than they do in sports pages. The 1936 Olympics were a rare event when the presence of athletics would highlight the atrocities that would go down in history.

In the early 1930s, Germany was suffering through its own Great Depression. The country's economy was dependent on both foreign capital—mostly from the United States—and on foreign trade. When foreign investment and trade stopped, the German middle class was thrown into economic despair. This opened many of its citizens to extremist ideas. In the 1932 German elections, Adolf Hitler's National Socialist German Workers' Party (Nazi Party) had won many seats in the legislature, and he was eventually appointed as chancellor. In less than a year, he would use his power to form a dictatorship, passing acts that gave him full control over the legislative and executive branches of the government. By July 1933, the Nazi Party was declared the only legal political party in Germany.

The day before the president died, Hitler's cabinet enacted a law that abolished the office of the president and combined the powers with those of the chancellor. With that passage, Hitler became head of state and government with supreme command over the armed forces. He began to mobilize the military and announced a massive expansion. Hitler focused on developing the depressed country, putting unemployed countrymen to work to build the first superhighways, called autobahns, which had no speed limit. Nazi Germans created hydrogen-filled zeppelins, or airships that were the length of three football fields. He implemented strict schooling programs that focused on both education and a physically fit youth. He even promoted anti-smoking campaigns and abstinence from alcohol and meat, stating German bodies should be kept clean of intoxicating or unclean substances.

What he's more known for, of course, is the disposal of what he considered an "unclean" people. New laws banned marriage and extramarital intercourse between non-Jewish and Jewish Germans. Hitler was a proponent of eugenics, which is the belief that the human species could be improved by discouraging reproduction of people who have genetic defects or perceived undesirable traits, and then encouraging reproduction of people with inheritable desirable traits. His early targets were children with physical and developmental disabilities; he created a euthanasia program to kill disabled adults. He focused his efforts on growing the "pure" Aryan race, those with fair skin, light hair, and light eyes.

Jesse Owens was aware of the sentiments of Hitler and the Nazi Party. "The greetings I received in the German capital had been bittersweet," he wrote in *The Jesse Owens Story*. "There were cheering crowds for me when I got off the train. But then I saw newspapers which told of hated American 'black auxiliary tribes' of which I was supposed to be the leader.

"German's leader and host of the games, Adolf Hitler, had made some stronger statements against the Negro athletes from the United States who were to compete. Hitler believed that his 'Aryan' race—blond, blue-eyed 'supermen'—were meant to rule the earth. Negroes seemed to be the most opposite to the Aryan type, and the German dictator openly called them an inferior race.

"I'd never had time to be a crusader. But when the hour came for me to compete, I was mad. I was angry because of the insults that Hitler and the other German leaders hurled at me and my Negro teammates on the Olympic squad. I was angry for all the colored people back home who had to work and slave to give me and those few others a chance for fame and a better life."

One month into office, Hitler ordered the creation of fifty concentration camps to imprison "enemies of the state." Within four months, those concentration camps would imprison twenty-seven thousand people, mostly Jews and communists, in brutal, nearly unlivable conditions. Between 1939 and 1945, Nazis and their collaborators were responsible for the deaths of between eleven million and fourteen million people, including about six million Jews—two-thirds of the Jewish population in Europe.

While the worst was yet to come to Nazi Germany, outsiders began to grasp the atrocities taking place. As the Olympic Games approached, many were disgusted by their location. An American columnist, Westbrook Pegler, wrote: "Germany was awarded these games four years ago. But that was another Germany. At that time the international body which selected the site acted on the supposition that certain essential sporting conditions could be guaranteed this year. If the committee had had any idea that four years later the games would be used to ballyhoo Adolf Hitler and to endorse a regime of murder, persecution and paganism, the program would have been awarded to another country," according to *Triumph*.

An evil dictator he may have been, but Hitler also was smart. He knew his Germany ought to put its best foot forward during the Olympics, in an attempt to quell all the dissent coming from outsiders. Hitler ordered that visible discrimination against Jews, as well as arrests of German residents who were opposed to Nazism, should cease. Hitler's personal architect Albert Speer wrote, "He gave orders that everything should be done to convey the impression of a peace-minded Germany to the many prominent foreign guests," according to Jesse Owens. The attention paid to the Olympic experience also was impressive, particularly through the use of advanced technology. New to the 1936 Olympics were advanced measuring devices, high-speed cameras to help determine the outcomes of track and swimming races, electronic scoreboards, and a sensing device for fencing. The Berlin Olympics also were to be the first televised Games, through a small local network. A stadium had been built with the capacity to seat 110,000, and the indoor swimming pool held 20,000 people.

American novelist Thomas Wolfe said omens for the brutality that was to come could be found in the Games. "There seemed to be something ominous in [the pageantry]," he wrote. "One sensed a stupendous concentration of effort, a tremendous drawing together and ordering in the vast collective power of the whole land. And the thing that made it seem ominous was that it so evidently went beyond what the Games themselves demanded. The Games were overshadowed, and were no longer merely sporting competitions to which other nations had sent their chosen teams. They became, day after day, an orderly and overwhelming demonstration in which the whole of Germany had been schooled and disciplined. It was as if the Games had been chosen as a symbol of the new collective might, a means of showing to the world in concrete terms what this new [Nazi] power had come to be."

While Hitler expected Aryan dominance, the German people were fascinated by Owens, hounding him for autographs, interviews, and handshakes. Ohio State coach Larry Snyder warned Owens not to focus on the attention as an ego boost, thinking he may lose his competitive edge. Owens, always pleasant in demeanor, played to the crowds but kept enough distance to maintain his edge. He also

Adolf Hitler (*front left*) congratulated only the winners who fit into his beliefs of the human ideal.

did not lose sight of the opinions of the man in charge. In his autobiography, he wrote: "We were everything Hitler hated. In particular, Hitler hated my skin." Owens credited Ralph Metcalfe, his longtime rival and Olympic teammate, for calming the fears of the African Americans on the team. They were urged not to take the bait or comment on Hitler or the Nazis; they were there to win gold medals.

Sunday, August 2, was the first day of competition. A member of the German team won the shot put and was then invited into Hitler's presidential box for a congratulatory handshake. Three Finnish athletes swept the 10,000-meter (10,936 yd) run and German women took gold and silver in the javelin; Hitler offered personal congratulations to all of them. The congratulations ceased when an African American, Cornelius Johnson, won the high jump. The president of the International Olympic Committee warned Hitler that he could not show favoritism in which gold medalists he chose to recognize—it was to be all or none. Hitler chose "none." He famously left the stadium before the American national anthem could be played, a snub that was played out in many American headlines. In the *New York Times*, Arthur Daley wrote, "Five minutes before the United States jumpers moved in for the ceremony of the Olympic triumph, Hitler left his box. Press box interpreters of this step chose to put two and two together and arrive at the figure four. In this they may be correct."

That same day, Owens's pursuit of his Olympic dream was under way. He was slotted to run in the twelfth heat of the 100-meter-dash qualifiers, which gave him an opportunity to scope out the competition before his own race. As he used his silver souvenir trowel to scoop out the starting holes for his feet (starting blocks did not exist at the time) in the cinder track, he noticed the recent rains had damaged the track, making for less-than-optimum conditions for a record-setting run. Yet, he finished in 10.2 seconds, which would have been a world record, had officials not ruled the run "wind-aided." Events are ruled wind-aided when wind speeds are above certain levels. Today, times or distances cannot be considered for a record if there was a tailwind of more than 2.0 meters per second (2.2 yards per second) in a dash or jump performance.

The semifinals and finals were the next day, and the track was in even worse shape. After breezing through the semifinals, Owens was assigned the first lane, which was especially treacherous, for the finals. "I was looking at the finish line," Owens said, "and realizing that five of the world's fastest humans wanted to beat me to it." Journalist Eleanor Holm Jarrett recalled the nonchalance with which Owens approached the race. "Jesse gave me the day's laugh when he shook hands with another runner before starting," she wrote. "It strikes me he must have been saying goodbye before departing on his fast journey." Halfway through the race, Owens already had a full-yard lead on his closest competitor. He won the race in 10.3 seconds, tying an Olympic and world record. With Hitler watching from his presidential box, the crowd chanted Owens's name as he jogged a victory lap around the track.

The story of what happened next has been reported, changed, disputed, and then perhaps changed again. Most eyewitness accounts state Hitler exchanged a wave with Owens after he left the Olympic medals podium. Years later, Owens would state that wave never took place. Even with the truth somewhat obscured, it was abundantly clear that Hitler would not be offering congratulatory handshakes. Baldur von Schirach, the leader of the Nazi Youth who, in 1946, was convicted of conspiring to commit crimes against humanity, suggested Hitler allow himself to be photographed with Owens. According to *Triumph*, Hitler would respond with outrage: "The Americans ought to be ashamed of themselves for letting their medals be won by Negroes," he said. "I myself would never shake hands with one of them." A handshake, of course, was not what Jesse

Jesse Owens (*center*) won the gold medal in the long jump, besting German Carl Ludwig "Luz" Long (*right*), who would become a great friend.

Owens came to Berlin for. He had one gold medal hanging around his neck and plans to earn more.

Tuesday, August 4, was Owens's busiest day at the Olympics, with the first-round and quarterfinal races for the 200 meters; and the first round, semifinals, and finals in the long jump. Owens started the day with an Olympic record of 21.1 seconds in the 200-meter qualifiers. As he headed to the pit for the long-jump competition, he found himself in a duel with the German Carl Ludwig "Luz" Long, whose features and athletic physique embodied the Aryan ideal. To qualify for the semifinals, a mark of 23 feet, 5.5 inches (7.15 m) needed to be leapt—a distance Owens had been regularly surpassing since high school. The pressure seemed light. Owens started his **run through**, a customary jog down the runway done by American jumpers, but unfamiliar to the European officials. A **foul** was called, meaning Owens would be listed as having attempted one jump already, with two left. The normally unflappable Owens began thinking too much. In his second attempt, he was measuring each **stride** in his head, leading to a wobbly jump of 23 feet 3 inches (7.09 m)—two inches (0.05 m) short of qualifying and a laughable effort for the world record-holder. (Other accounts state Owens fouled on his second attempt, as well.)

Kicking himself for leaving just one chance to make it to the semifinals, Owens related later he felt a tap on his shoulder. In a thick and strange accent, Owens heard: "What has taken your goat, Jazzee Owenz?" The voice belonged to Luz Long, who then said. "I think I know what is wrong

Jesse Owens credited German Carl Ludwig "Luz" Long with helping him overcome a poor start in the long-jump qualifiers; the two were inseparable for much of the Olympics.

with you. … You know, you should be able to qualify with your eyes closed. Why do you not draw a line a few inches in back of the board and aim at making yourself take off from there? You'll be sure not to foul, and you certainly ought to jump far enough to qualify." The messages and sportsmanship struck Owens. When he landed in the sand after his third attempt, he knew he had qualified. Long was there to pat Owens on the back and to say: "See, it was easy."

The rest of the afternoon, Owens and Long were locked in a head-to-head battle for the gold medal at a long-jump pit right underneath Hitler's box. The Olympic record fell with nearly each leap, as each man pushed the other to unthinkable distances. Long set an Olympic record in his first jump of the finals with a distance of 25 feet, 9¾ inches (7.86 m). Owens then tied the mark with his first jump. With his second jump, Owens exceeded 26 feet (7.93 m). Long couldn't match him. The German's leg was throbbing with pain, and Owens recalls rubbing Long with liniment for about ten minutes while Hitler glared at both of them from the sidelines. Long fouled on his final attempt. Owens, meanwhile, used his last attempt to set an Olympic record of 26 feet, 5½ inches (8.06 m), which would hold for twenty-four years. Long was the first to embrace Owens.

"I was the winner," Owens wrote in *The Jesse Owens Story*. "In a more important way, though, *he* was the winner. He had done his best—and without him I never could have done *my* best. Luz truly showed the spirit of the Olympics, something that will last a lot more than twenty-four years." Owens also remarked at the gumption of Long to congratulate him right under Hitler's nose. "It took a lot of courage for him to befriend me in front of Hitler," Owens said, according to *ESPN*. "You can melt down all the medals and cups I have and they wouldn't be a plating on the 24-karat friendship I felt for Luz Long at that moment. Hitler must have gone crazy watching us embrace."

Owens and Long were inseparable for the rest of the Olympics, spending late nights talking together in the Olympic village. Both had come from poor families, and both had a wife and children at home. They spoke about their passion for their sport and the challenges that came with it. They considered the racial prejudice in both Germany and the United States. Long would ultimately fight for Germany in World War II, though Owens said he knew Long did so without believing "any of that 'Aryan superiority' nonsense Hitler spouted," he wrote in *The Jesse Owens Story*. "He never would have helped me in the broad jump if he'd believed it." Owens and Long wrote letters to one another for years after the Olympics until Long stopped responding. Long's wife confirmed he had been killed in the war. In *Blackthink*, Owens wrote he and Long both had "the priceless knowledge that the only bond worth anything between human beings is their humanness."

With two gold medals secured, Owens woke up the next day prepared for battle in the 200 meters—though slightly tired from his late-night conversing with Long. Despite the rain, Owens breezed through the semifinals with a date in the evening finals waiting. Mack Robinson, the older brother of Jackie Robinson, who would break the color barrier in baseball, had tied Owens's record of 21.1 seconds in the semifinals, proving a worthy contender. But Owens, known for his quick starts, blasted off the starting line and ultimately won the finals in a world record time of 20.7 seconds. "Owens looked like a dark streak of lightning," wrote famed journalist Grantland Rice. "His final performance in breaking all records for 200 meters under miserable conditions, with a rain-soaked track, left the athletes of fifty-one nations goggle-eyed with astonishment."

The skies opened shortly after, and Owens received his third gold medal under a sheet of rain and wild applause. (Hitler had already left the stadium.) Owens had been slated to compete in three events, and he would head home with a gold medal for each effort. Joe Williams wrote in his column for the August 6 *New York World-*

The reconfigured 400-meter sprint relay team of Jesse Owens, Ralph Metcalfe, Foy Draper, and Frank Wykoff breezed to a gold medal.

USA
USA

Telegram: "Jesse Owens's Olympics ended yesterday. Today the Olympics take on the international form for which they were originally designed. Which is to say some of the athletes in other countries will get a chance to break into the headlines. Up to now it has been all Owens. The Ohio Negro has been the whole show."

Owens met with reporters after the 200 meters and called Hitler's early departure "immaterial" but spoke of his sadness that his Olympic experience, four days in, was to be over. "I'm just getting the feel of the track," he said, according to *Triumph*. "I never was in better condition and would like to keep competing. I told Coach [Lawson] Robertson I'd gladly run the relay if he wanted me. I hope there's a chance that they will keep me busy the rest of the week. I'm having a wonderful time."

In a controversial decision that would be discussed for decades, Owens earned the opportunity to continue his wonderful time. Robertson would call on Owens to compete in the 400-meter (437 yd) sprint relay, in what he deemed at the time was a move purely based on talent. He told one reporter "the Germans quietly have built up a quartet which had been clocked in sensational time," according to *Triumph*. "I'd like to let everybody run, but we're here to win as many events as possible. They are likely to criticize any decision I may make, but my job's to put the best possible teams in the race." Those attuned to the track world were less critical of this stance but more questioning of the fact Robertson seemed to have changed his philosophy. If he was looking for the best possible team, Owens always would have been on it. In fact, Robertson had excluded Metcalfe and Eddie Tolan, the two best sprinters, in the 1932 Olympics, and an all-white American team competed in the race.

Skin hue wouldn't be the point of contention this time around. First the question arose: whose place would Owens take on the relay team? Would it be Metcalfe, who was competing in his final Olympics and therefore would never have another opportunity to race for a medal? Frank Wykoff, who finished fourth in the 100 meters and would thus be returning home with no medals to show for his efforts this time, despite having won gold for the 1928 and 1932 relay teams? Or would the excluded runner be Foy Draper, Sam Stoller, or Marty Glickman, who had trained with the team all year?

The final team was announced as Owens, Metcalfe, Wykoff, and Draper. Robertson told Stoller and Glickman: "We were hoping to give you both a chance, but we can't afford to take the Germans lightly. We have reasons to believe that they've been hiding their best runners, waiting to upset us." No one believed Robertson's rationale, and Glickman was quick to call him out. "Coach, this is ridiculous," Glickman said, according to *Triumph*. "You don't hide world-class sprinters. They have to get race experience. Any American relay team you pick will win by fifteen yards [13.7 meters]—*any* of our runners, the milers or the hurdlers, could run against the Germans or anyone else and win by fifteen yards.

Glickman Left Out

Marty Glickman had a long and outstanding career as a broadcaster but believed he'd be remembered as an athlete only for not running in the Olympics.

"If it hadn't been for that decision by our coaches, no one would remember me as an Olympian," he told an interviewer in 1996, according to his January 4, 2001, obituary in the *New York Times*. "I mean, name another 400-meter relay runner. But I'd much prefer to have run and won a medal."

Glickman was a Bronx-born racer whose parents were Jewish immigrants. During high school in Brooklyn, Glickman was prominent and nationally dominating. He qualified for the Olympics while competing for the Syracuse University track team. Stoller, meanwhile, had grown up in Cincinnati, Ohio. He was one of the best sprinters the state had ever produced, but he was in Owens's shadow throughout his athletic career. Owens and Stoller raced on rival teams in high school, and then, as Owens went off to Ohio State, Stoller began racing for Michigan, a conference rival.

Glickman said Owens had mixed feelings about entering the race in place of his teammates, although his version of events differs from Owens's version. He recalled in a recording for the United States Holocaust Memorial Museum the events of the meeting in Berlin: "Jesse spoke up and said, 'Coach, I've won my three gold medals [the 100, the 200, and the long jump]. I'm tired. I've had it. Let Marty and Sam run, they deserve it,' said Jesse. And [assistant coach Dean] Cromwell pointed his finger at him and said, 'You'll do as you're told.' And in those days, black athletes did as they were told, and Jesse was quiet after that."

Glickman forcefully claimed over the years that Avery Brundage, President of the American Olympic Association (later named the **United States Olympic Committee**), and Cromwell were members of the First America Committee, which later advocated against US involvement in World War II, and were sympathetic to the Nazis. There are others who feel Brundage pressured Robertson to take the two Jewish runners out of the race so as to appease Hitler and avoid a situation in which Jewish athletes would be on the medal podium. Two years after the games, Hitler contracted Brundage's construction company to build the German embassy in Washington, DC.

Marty Glickman was excluded from the 400-meter sprint relay team in a controversial decision.

Glickman served as radio announcer for the New York Knicks of the NBA, the New York Giants and the New York Jets of the NFL, for major league baseball pregame and postgame shows, for track meets, and for Yonkers Raceway. He was hired by NBC to critique and train its announcers, but the hurt of not running in Berlin stayed with him.

The *Times* said that he wrote in 1994 about returning to Berlin in 1986 for the fiftieth anniversary of Owens winning four gold medals. "Suddenly a wave of rage overwhelmed me. I thought I was going to pass out. I began to scream every dirty curse word, every obscenity I knew. … being there, visualizing and reliving those moments, caused the eruption which had been gnawing at me for so long and which I thought I had expunged years ago."

If you drop us, there's going to be a helluva furor—we're the only two Jews on the track team."

Despite the consternation over the politics or discrimination that may have gone into the decision, one truth was clear: Owens would have the chance to achieve the ultimate Olympic glory, matched only once before, to win four gold medals. The Americans won their qualifying heat, as did the Germans and Dutch in theirs. The sprinters for the other countries, however, were the usual suspects. "The heralded Dutch and German opposition, which Head Coach Lawson Robertson said prompted him to use Owens and Draper, failed to materialize," wrote the Associated Press.

The afternoon hours led to soul-searching for Owens, on all accounts. He donned a pair of sunglasses and attempted to blend into the crowds while watching the decathlon championship. The disguise didn't work, and he was still hounded for autographs and pictures, despite the shifting moods taking place below the surface. Snyder, Owens's Ohio State coach, attempted to assuage the guilt Owens was feeling. "You've got no reason to feel bad about this," Snyder told him, according to *Triumph*. "If you were white, Robertson and Cromwell would never have considered *not* putting you on the relay. Remember when Stoller and Glickman get home, they'll have plenty of opportunities. Glickman's only eighteen. Jesse, these are your games, you're a competitor. You deserve that gold medal tomorrow."

Owens ran the first leg of the race, handing the baton off to Metcalfe with a 5-yard (4.6 m) lead. Metcalfe built on that lead, handing the baton off to Draper with a 7-yard

(6.4 m) lead. Journalist Paul Gallico wrote of Owens and Metcalfe's start: "The white boys to whom they turned over the baton could have crawled in on their hands and knees." The American team won the race by more than 12 yards (11 m) in a record-breaking 39.8 seconds. Owens earned his fourth gold medal, setting three world records along the way.

Germany won the overall medal competition, with a total of thirty-three gold medals. The United States finished second, having dominated the track and field events. The level of joy Hitler experienced at the German victories was perhaps only matched by the level of displeasure he felt at Owens's success. "[Hitler] followed the athletic contests with great excitement," wrote Albert Speer, according to *Jesse Owens*. "Each of the German victories—and there were a surprising number of these—made him happy, but he was highly annoyed by the series of triumphs by the marvelous colored American runner, Jesse Owens. People whose antecedents came from the jungle were primitive, Hitler said with a shrug; their physiques were stronger than those of civilized whites. They represented unfair competition and hence must be excluded from future games."

Two days after the closing ceremonies in Berlin, the Olympic Village became an infantry training center. The largest restaurant and hospitals in Germany were transformed into a military hospital. One dining hall and lounge became an officers' club. Athletes slow to leave their dormitories heard the noise of machine guns from nearby training fields. World War II would put an end to any talk of a 1940 or 1944 Olympics. He didn't know it at the time, but Owens's Olympic career was over.

Jesse Owens raced a horse in Havana, Cuba, to earn money after the Olympics were over.

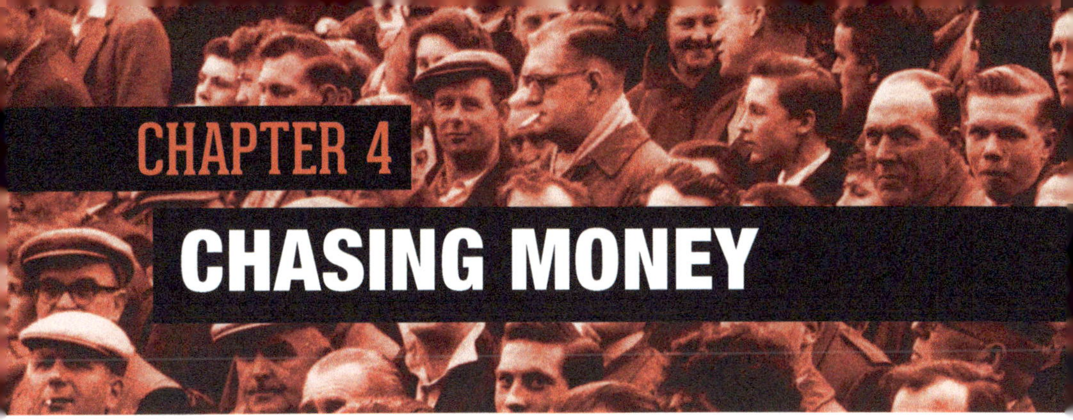

CHAPTER 4

CHASING MONEY

"There were four gold medals on the broken-down dresser in our bedroom, an oak tree next to the closet, and no money in my wallet."

—Jesse Owens in *The Jesse Owens Story*

Jesse Owens was a household name across the world. Newspapers in the southern United States that typically ignored African-American athletes had Owens's photo on their pages. For two weeks, his name appeared on a Broadway marquee, as movie houses showed tape of his Olympic success. A German publication even called Owens the *Wunderathlet* of the Berlin Games.

But even as the Olympics came to a close, Owens's travels were not over. In order to fund their Olympic venture, the AAU had agreed for its athletes to compete in exhibition meets across Europe following the Olympics. In order for Owens and the other athletes to maintain their amateur standing, they would be paid nothing. Instead of heading home to his family, Owens was shuttled around Europe as the main attraction. His presence offered literal value to the AAU, as venue organizers offered higher percentages of gate receipts if Owens were to participate.

Owens was not happy about this obligation. Emotionally, he missed his wife and child and wished to get home to them. Physically, he was exhausted, having competed in fourteen total races, including qualifiers. Also, financially, offers were on the table to make him a rich man that would have to wait. The day after his relay race, Owens received a telegram from the California orchestra offering $25,000 just for introducing songs on stage for two weeks. Eddie Cantor offered $40,000 for Owens to participate in his vaudeville shows for ten weeks. Agents were calling from Hollywood and New York, wanting the star to be part of their productions.

Before going on the exhibition tour, it seemed Owens had begun to develop a clearer picture of his future. "I'm anxious to finish my college career, but I can't afford to miss this chance if it really means big money," he told a reporter, according to *Jesse Owens: An American Life.* "I can always go back and get a degree." Larry Snyder, his college coach, would not hold him back. "It would be foolish for me to stand in Jesse's way," Snyder said. "He's absolutely at the height of his fame now. Nothing that he could do in his remaining year at college competition would lift him to a higher peak in the athletic world than he now enjoys."

Owens was ready to get home to start sorting through his options. Instead, he was boarding a train to Cologne, Germany, to perform for thirty-five thousand spectators. Owens was hardly himself, having lost 10 pounds (4.5 kilograms) and struggling to concentrate. He won the long jump modestly with a leap of 24 feet 4½ inches (7.32 m), though he lost in the 100 meters to Ralph

In one of his post-Olympic appearances, Jesse Owens joined dancer Bill "Bojangles" Robinson and some chorus girls on stage at New York's Cotton Club.

Metcalfe. Owens admitted later to Snyder that he just didn't care. The meet lasted until 8:30 p.m. and was followed by a banquet that didn't end until midnight. The next morning, Owens was on a flight to Prague, Czechoslovakia, where he would run that same night. Owens won his events but ran the 100 meters in his slowest time in months and leapt a distance he was jumping in high school. Next came a meet in Bochum, Germany, where he tied his own world record in the 100 meters but jumped an abysmal 23 feet, 3/8th inches (7.01 m), and was beaten by an unknown German athlete by almost a foot.

The athletes were next shepherded to London, where Owens's aggravation peaked. He competed in the 400-meter relay race, then blurted out at a press conference:

"I'm burned out, I'm busted, and I'm tired of being treated like cattle. I know how hard it is for a member of my race to make money … and I have to reach for it while it's being offered to me," according to *Jesse Owens*. That relay would be Owens's last as an amateur athlete.

Avery Brundage, the American Olympic Association president, told Snyder that Owens would face "dire consequences" if he did not go to Stockholm to compete in the next exhibition meet in Sweden. Owens chanced it and boarded a ship for the United States. Meanwhile, the AAU announced Owens would be suspended from all further competition in the United States due to his failure "to fulfill his competitive obligations," according to *Jesse Owens: An American Life*. Owens made a public statement in response, saying: "This suspension is very unfair to me. There's nothing I can gain out of this trip [to Sweden]. All we athletes get out of this Olympic business is a view out of a train or airplane window. It gets tiresome, it really does. This track business is becoming one of the biggest rackets in the world. It doesn't mean a darned thing to us athletes. The AAU gets the money. It gets all the money collected in the United States and then comes over to Europe and takes half the proceeds. A fellow desires something for himself."

Back in America, Owens went on something of a victory tour, where he was greeted with applause as his ship docked at the New York harbor. He then returned to Cleveland so his hometown fans could greet him, then Columbus for another victory procession and more speeches. Three weeks after the Olympics ended, Owens slept in his own bed once again.

To help him sift through the offers on the table, Owens hired Marty Forkins as his agent after being introduced to him by dancer and movie star Bill "Bojangles" Robinson. Then the opportunities began disappearing. Eddie Cantor backed out, as did the California orchestra. Talks of movie deals faded. Having lost his amateur status, Owens could no longer race, either. He began to understand the harsh realities of the moment, saying, "After I came home from the 1936 Olympics with my four medals, it became increasingly apparent that everyone was going to slap me on the back, want to shake my hand or have me up to their suite. But no one was going to offer me a job," according to *Jesse Owens: Champion Athlete*.

Owens amassed enough odd jobs to make a living for himself and his family, though it meant being on the road constantly. He attended banquets, made appearances on radio broadcasts, endorsed clothing or foods. Each stop earned him about $1,000, certainly enough combined to pay the bills. His biggest paycheck came in his campaigning for Republican presidential candidate Alf Landon. Why get involved in politics? Little convincing was needed when Landon reminded him that President Franklin Delano Roosevelt had not even sent him a telegram of congratulations following his Olympic victories. Owens earned between $10,000 and $15,000 for those speaking appearances—enough to buy a car, a house for his parents, clothes and jewelry for his wife, and a down payment on

Jesse Owens was celebrated with a parade down Broadway in New York City upon his return home from the 1936 Olympics.

Welcome Olympian

a car for Charles Riley, his first track coach. While many would argue he never had the one big endorsement deal to classify him as rich, like modern-day athletes, Owens's income during the Great Depression era was remarkable. In 1936, four out of five Americans earned less than $2,000, and African Americans earned less still, according to *Jesse Owens: An American Life*. Less than 1 percent of Americans made more than $10,000 that year.

In December 1936, Owens was named the Associated Press Athlete of the Year. He was only the second African-American winner, boxer Joe Louis having been recognized the previous year. Owens would find a way to race one more time that year. Originally, he was scheduled to run against Cuba's fastest athlete: Conrado Rodriques. But the AAU intervened, warning Rodriques he would be banned from amateur competition in the United States if he ran against the "professional" Owens. The threat scared off Rodriques, and Forkins, Owens's agent, pitched the idea of Owens running "against time" during the halftime of a soccer game in Havana, Cuba. Then, a third idea arose: Owens would race a thoroughbred horse named Julio McCaw. Owens received a 40-yard (37 m) head start and $2,000 for what would ultimately be a several-yard victory.

Owens responded to this spectacle experience with a mix of emotions. Initially, after the race, he told two reporters, according to *Jesse Owens: An American Life*: "Since I haven't competed for a long time, and considering the condition of the track, I am satisfied with my showing. I would be willing to race a horse without a handicap,

Jesse Owens's widow, Ruth (*center*), was present in 1984 at the renaming of a street in Berlin after her husband.

even from scratch provided the animal selected is not remarkably fast. … It sure feels good to get out on the cinders again." Years later, upon reflection, he presented a different attitude, more of desperation. "People said it was degrading for an Olympic champion to run against a horse, but what was I supposed to do?" Owens asked an interviewer, according to *Jesse Owens: An American Life*. "I had four gold medals, but you can't eat four gold medals. There was no television, no big advertising, no endorsements then. Not for a black man, anyway."

Owens's attempt to profit from his Olympic success rubbed many writers and officials the wrong way. The James E. Sullivan trophy, which is given to the year's best amateur athlete, did not go to Owens in 1936. He finished in second place in the voting behind Olympic decathlete Glenn Morris. Roi Ottley of the *Amsterdam News* posed several questions that allude to the reason for the voters' decision, according to *Jesse Owens: An American Life*: Has he upheld the amateur code? Does his character promise success as a leader and force for good in the community? In what vocation is he now engaged? In considering how those questions might be answered, Ottley surmised: "Our feeling is he might flunk."

Owens's skin color was a presumed barrier to consistent financial security. Journalist Paul Gallico reflected on the dichotomous role of the African-American athlete, saying he was a "full-fledged citizen, and a true American" when he was a college football star or in the midst of his Olympic victory tour. "At other times," Gallico wrote, according to *Jesse Owens: An American Life*, "he remains just plain [black man], and we'd rather he weren't around, because he represents a social problem."

Owens approached new ventures as an entertainer. In January 1937, he signed a contract with Consolidated Radio Artists of New York City to lead a touring twelve-piece band of African-American musicians, primarily announcing the songs before they were to be performed, but sometimes taking on a singing role as well. Owens later recalled his inability to carry a tune. The travel also began to wear on him, and by April he had quit the band.

Up next was a try at a different athletic career: basketball. Owens assembled a professional basketball squad he named the Olympians. They played against local amateur clubs and college teams, with Owens often providing some sort of halftime exhibition of running skill and speed. His long-running difference of opinion with the AAU, however, would interject into this new undertaking, too. The AAU stated that any team participating in amateur events could not profit from being on tour; college squads were barred from playing against the Olympians, and the team had disbanded by the following spring.

The next two years were financially bleak for Owens, who worked for a time as a playground director and opened a dry-cleaning business with two partners. The business struggled, and Owens took little interest. He ultimately found himself filing for bankruptcy, unable to

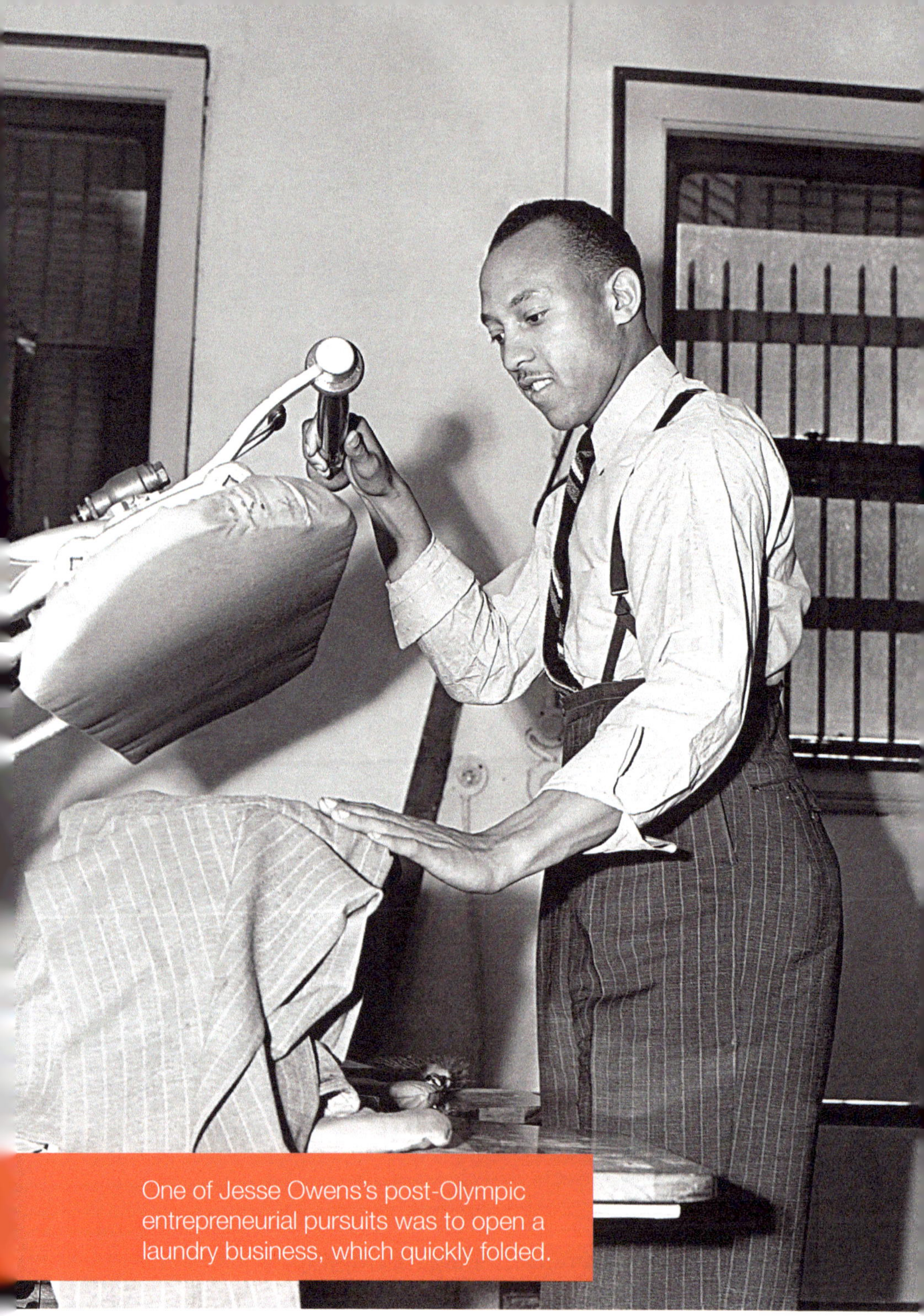

One of Jesse Owens's post-Olympic entrepreneurial pursuits was to open a laundry business, which quickly folded.

pay off the loans on the laundry equipment. Then, the Internal Revenue Services (IRS) came looking for him, as he had not paid taxes on $20,000 he had earned after the Berlin Olympics.

To pay back his debts and start building a bank account again, Owens continued with his exhibition running. Throughout the summer of 1939, he traveled with the Indianapolis Clowns and Toledo Crawfords, Negro League baseball teams that played in the Midwest and South. After each game, Owens would race against the fastest man in town. His opponents were offered a 10-yard (9.1 m) head start, and he still beat them all. But he did not feel fulfilled. He was drifting aimlessly from one exhibition or playing field to another, missing out on valuable time with his family. In 1940, after Owens's parents had both died, he returned to Columbus to be with his wife and children. He re-enrolled at Ohio State and accepted a position as an assistant track coach. Owens spent three full semesters at Ohio State but consistently struggled with his classwork. In December 1941, Owens left the school for good, with a 1.5 grade point average and without a diploma. That same month, Japan bombed the US air and naval base at Pearl Harbor, Hawaii, and America would enter World War II.

As the head of a household, Owens was not required to serve in the military, but he would participate in American military activities: the Civilian Defense Office asked for his assistance running a government fitness program. He gave speeches on fitness and health and initiated exercise

Jesse Owens joined Sargent Shriver (*center*) and baseball player Stan Musial to discuss youth fitness programs in 1964.

programs in African-American communities. During these travels, Owens learned of a job opportunity with the Ford Motor Company, as personnel manager for the overworked assembly line, which was churning out tanks, planes, guns, ammunition, and other wartime necessities. He would soon be promoted to Director of Negro Personnel at Ford's River Rouge plant. Through a staff reshuffling a couple years later, he was offered a lesser job that he chose not to accept.

After the war ended, Owens was back on the travel circuit with the Harlem Globetrotters and the Cincinnati Crescents, signing autographs, giving speeches, and running world-record times over short distances. He was away from his family for weeks at a time; he moved them to Chicago, leaving behind their friends and much of their comfort. But the next few years would mark success for Owens, who spent time appearing on radio programs, working as a master of ceremonies at banquets or sporting events, and writing a column for the *Chicago Defender*, an African-American publication. As a respected member of the Chicago community, he earned roles as the secretary of the Illinois State Athletic Commission and later the Illinois Youth Athletic Commission, which organized recreational programs and athletic events throughout the state. He also was asked to represent the United States as a goodwill ambassador during a tour of Asia, where he spread the message of economic and political freedom, while also leading running clinics.

In 1956, Owens attended the Summer Olympic Games in Melbourne, Australia, as a personal representative of President Dwight D. Eisenhower. There, he saw his records fall to American Bobby Morrow, aside from his long-jump leap, which would be bested in the 1960 Games.

GAME-CHANGING CHRONOLOGY

September 12, 1913: Born James Cleveland Owens in Oakville, Alabama.

August 1922: The Owens family moves to Cleveland, Ohio.

April 1928: Owens sets schoolboy records in the high jump and long jump under lifelong mentor Charles Riley.

August 1932: Owens becomes a father for the first time.

November 1932: Owens is elected president of his senior class and captain of the track team.

Spring 1933: Owens ties the world record in the 100-yard dash and breaks the world record in the 220-yard dash at the National Interscholastic Meet.

October 1933: Owens enrolls at Ohio State University.

May 25, 1935: Owens ties the world record in the 100-yard dash and sets world records in the 220-yard dash, long jump, and 220-yard low hurdles in less than an hour.

August 1936: Owens competes in the Berlin Olympic Games, where he wins four gold medals.

December 1936: Owens becomes ineligible to compete for Ohio State, due to being stripped of his amateur status after refusing to continue competing in international exhibition meets following the Olympics; runs a race against a horse in Havana, Cuba.

1937: Owens becomes a bandleader and the owner of a basketball team, softball team, and dry-cleaning company.

February 1939: Owens files for personal bankruptcy.

October 1940: Owens returns to Ohio State University but does not have the grades to obtain his degree.

January 1942: Owens is appointed the Director of National Fitness by the US Office of Civilian Defense.

July 1950: Owens is named the greatest track athlete of the past half-century by the Associated Press.

December 1953: Owens is appointed secretary of the Illinois State Athletic Commission.

July 1955: Owens travels to Asia for a goodwill tour, promoting economic and political freedom while giving running clinics.

Summer 1956: Owens attends the Summer Olympics as a personal representative of President Dwight D. Eisenhower.

Summer 1965: Owens works as a running coach for the New York Mets.

June 1972: Owens is awarded an honorary doctorate from Ohio State University.

October 1973: Owens is appointed to the US Olympic Committee board of directors.

January 1974: Owens is inducted into the US Track and Field Hall of Fame.

January 1976: Owens receives the Presidential Medal of Freedom from President Gerald Ford.

March 31, 1980: Owens dies at the age of sixty-six.

During an awards ceremony at the 1968 Olympics in Mexico City, Tommie Smith (*center*) and John Carlos (*right*) protested racial discrimination with a black power salute.

CHAPTER 5

OWENS, TIMES CHANGE

"I know I'll drop in my tracks someday. And I won't really mind if it comes sooner than it should, as long as I'm making tracks when I drop."

—Jesse Owens in *I Have Changed*

No matter where he went, or whether or not he was in an official ambassador role, Owens continuously promoted the message of the American Dream. He stated on several occasions that he saw himself first as an American and second as an African American. He opposed the tactics of the Black Panthers, a revolutionary group that fought for African-American rights. Owens stood strong on the belief that one could succeed through hard work and perseverance, regardless of skin color.

His stance was tested in 1968, when African-American athletes joined a growing movement to boycott the Olympic Games. It was sought as a protest of the ongoing racism in the United States, the country's involvement in the Vietnam War, and the participation of an Olympic team from South Africa, where discriminatory practices were the rule under apartheid. Owens spoke publicly against the boycott, stating the Olympic Games were the preeminent platform for African Americans to close the gap between themselves and their white counterparts.

The Americans ultimately would compete. The Games would partially be remembered for the show of protest by American sprinters Tommie Smith and John Carlos, who raised black-gloved fists toward the sky while on the podium during the national anthem. Smith defended the action, saying: "The fact is the fight for rights among blacks is bigger than the winning of any one event in sports. I used victory as a means to an end, which will be reached when blacks have reached equal status in society," according to *Jesse Owens*. While the world was stirring over the demonstration, Owens met with the sprinters, trying to persuade them to apologize. Smith and Carlos refused and were suspended from the team.

Owens was inspired by this incident to begin work on an autobiography called *Blackthink: My Life as Black Man and White Man*. In it, he wrote about the American dream. He implored African Americans to search inward for the causes of their despair rather than blame discrimination. He wrote harshly against the militants, who were using force to achieve the passing of their message. "Sometimes they'll talk with you," he wrote in *Blackthink*. "But in the background is the gun and the knife, the riot and the revolution. … Even if the militants were right about every single thing they advocate, the means they're using and threatening to use to win their ends would make it all worthless."

There was an outcry from the African-American community. Had Owens forgotten what racism was like? Had he completely lost touch with the trials and

Gerald Ford recognized Jesse Owens with the Presidential Medal of Freedom in 1976.

tribulations still taking place in America? Owens grew introspective, considering the criticism and condemnation he was receiving. He quickly began work on another book project: *I Have Changed*. He acknowledged the struggles that he and his family experienced and acknowledged that barriers still existed for African Americans in the United States. He still maintained his stance, however, that opportunity is accessible to everyone.

Despite his fickle pursuits after his Olympic success in 1936, Jesse Owens nonetheless became a symbol for the opportunity that he so preached. His skin color may have kept him from getting the recognition he was long due, though it ultimately came.

In 1972, Owens was awarded an honorary degree from Ohio State as a doctor of athletic arts. Two years later, the NCAA gave him the Theodore Roosevelt Award for his achievements after leaving amateur athletics. That same year, he was inducted into the Track and Field Hall of Fame. The most notable honor came in 1976, forty years after his glory days. President Gerald Ford presented him with the Presidential Medal of Freedom, the highest civilian honor given by the US government, for serving as "a source of inspiration" for all Americans. Three years later, President Jimmy Carter recognized Owens with the Living Legends Award for his ability "to inspire others to reach for greatness."

More localized awards, however, had more meaning to Owens. In 1979, the city of Decatur, Alabama, invited him to appear as a guest of honor to receive the Audie Murphy Patriotism Award. A white mayor made the presentation just a few miles from Owens's birthplace.

Historians have been known to downplay the achievements of athletes in the realm of effecting social change, but Owens's success would resonate in the African-American community. An intellectual African-American magazine, *The Crisis*, wrote an editorial on the benefits reaped by the whole community because of the talents of Owens and boxer Joe Louis. "Those who maintain that a Negro historian or editor or philosopher or scientist or composer or singer or poet or painter is more important than a great athlete are on sound ground, but they would

Jesse Owens advises long jumper Bob Beamon of the University of Texas at El Paso at the 1968 NCAA track championships. At the Olympics later that year, Beamon surpassed the world record by a huge 1 foot, 9¾ inches (0.55 m).

Motivational Words

Many athletes would follow in Jesse Owens's footsteps by attempting to break world records on the track or in the long-jump pit. However, few would attempt the exact same feat as Owens in the Olympics by competing in the 100-meter dash, 200-meter dash, 4 × 100 relay, and long jump. Carl Lewis not only attempted to match Owens's accomplishments—he succeeded.

A chance meeting between Lewis and Owens took place at a track meet on Franklin Field in Philadelphia, Pennsylvania, when Lewis was a twelve-year-old boy and Owens was almost sixty. *New York Times* columnist Dave Anderson wrote that Lewis's father arranged for the introduction, telling Owens his son was a long jumper. Bill Lewis had met Owens when he was a teenager in Chicago.

"You're a long jumper?" Jesse Owens asked. "You must be a spunky little guy to be jumping against all these big guys."

Owens also told him: "Have fun running and jumping, but never overburden yourself with what you're trying to do."

Lewis credits Owens for springboarding his faith in himself.

"I was a little kid, I was a late bloomer and Jesse said, 'You're a little kid, but you can beat the big guys if you work hard.' It was a simple message but effective," Lewis told Yahoo Sports. "I never forgot that time, and it was kind of a bizarre situation because you look at this and say, 'You have got to be kidding me. I met Jesse when I was a kid' and growing up, watching the Olympics and loving it and wanting to go. And here I am later, being there in '84 and going there and trying to emulate someone I admire so much."

Lewis competed in four Olympic Games, from 1984 to 1996, and finished with nine gold medals and one silver. He was voted Sportsman of the Century by the International Olympic Committee in 1999.

Ruth Owens, Jesse's widow, presented the Jesse Owens International Trophy to Carl Lewis in 1985.

be foolish to maintain that these worthy individuals have more power for influence than the athletes," according to *The Legend of Jesse Owens*. "After all, it is not the infinitesimal intellectual American which needs a conversion on the race problem; it is the rank and file, the ones who never read a book by Du Bois, or heard a lecture by [NAACP leader] James Weldon Johnson, or scanned a poem of Countee Cullen, or heard a song by [opera contralto] Marian Anderson, or waded through a scholarly treatise. … For these millions, who hold the solution of the race problem in their hands, the beautiful breasting of a tape by Jesse Owens and the thud of a glove on the hand of Joe Louis carry more 'interracial education' than all the erudite philosophy ever written on race."

Owens's victories, however, were quick to illuminate the progress still necessary in the United States. He may have helped quash the German idea of Aryan dominance, but back on his home turf race relations were still very uneven. "When I came back to my native country, after all the stories about Hitler, I couldn't ride in the front of the bus," he said, according to ESPN. "I had to go to the back door. I couldn't live where I wanted. I wasn't invited to shake hands with Hitler, but I wasn't invited to the White House to shake hands with the President, either."

While his country would make progress throughout his life, Owens's stature grew with death. Owens died on March 31, 1980. He had been a pack-a-day cigarette smoker for thirty-five years and ultimately was hospitalized with an aggressive lung cancer that took his life in a matter of months.

Ohio State memorialized him by naming its athletic stadium after him. The following year, the Jesse Owens International Amateur Athletic Award was designated for the best amateur athlete in the world. A Jesse Owens Memorial Foundation was established to provide college scholarships to "needy but deserving youths." Additionally, a number of memorial track meets were run throughout the country, bearing his name. Perhaps surprisingly, Owens was recognized in a country that had seen his success but not welcomed it: Germany. One of the streets leading to the Olympic stadium in Berlin was renamed Jesse-Owens-Allee. A decade after Owens died, President George H. W. Bush posthumously awarded him the Congressional Medal of Honor. Bush called his victories in Berlin "an unrivaled athletic triumph, but more than that, a triumph for all humanity," according to ESPN.

Many contemporary athletes have reflected on the lessons of Owens and the message he left behind. Herb Douglas, a bronze medalist in the 1948 London Olympics, said Owens was "a role model, and led the way for so many of us to reach our goals," according to *Jesse Owens: An American Life*. "I'm sitting here because I had someone to try to emulate." Owens's unemployed cousin once said: "It makes me feel good on the inside what Jesse did. Even if I never made nothing of myself, I feel good that some of my people did."

The son of the late German Athlete Luz Long, Kai Long, and Luz's granddaughter Julia-Vanessa (*front left*) joined International Association of Athletics Federations president Lamine Diack and Jesse Owens's granddaughter, Marlene Dortch (*front right*), in honoring the long jumpers at the 2009 IAAF World Championships in Berlin.

asics
Australia

One African-American sociologist, Harry Edwards, warns against putting too much weight in the rags-to-riches story of Jesse Owens. He feared that Owens—and his accomplishments—would create a false sense of belief that poor but athletically gifted young African-American children could achieve social mobility through sports. Even Arthur Ashe, the famed African-American tennis star, cautioned against putting too much emphasis on athletics. "We have been on the same roads—sports and entertainment—too long," Ashe told the *New York Times*. "We need to pull over, fill up at the library, and speed away to Congress and the Supreme Court, the unions and the business world."

Regardless of how literally the story of Owens is read, one message seems to have carried through the years. He concluded *The Jesse Owens Story* by describing the vast technological changes he had seen in his life and how he saw hope for big changes in the hearts of humans: "Man has the free will to do anything he wants, if he just sets his whole spirit to it. Naturally, that isn't something you learn how to do in a day. Sometimes it can take a whole lifetime," he wrote. "But it's worth the struggle, believe me. I'm not just saying words—I *know*.

"And that's why I want to end the story of my life as I started it: by telling you that in America, anyone can still become somebody. That includes *you*."

Reading between the lines of Owens's story allows dreamers to keep dreaming. He saw all his records fall during his lifetime, but his accomplishments have yet to fade. The story of a young, sickly African-American boy developing into an Olympic champion despite discrimination at its most atrocious provides a message of the power of perseverance. As one journalist wrote: "We embrace it, for it reaffirms the human spirit and makes us believe we are still good, good enough to permit people to grow out of deprivation and make it to the top."

GLOSSARY

Amateur Athletic Union A nonprofit sports organization dedicated to the promotion and development of nonprofessional sports and physical fitness programs. It certifies athletes as amateurs and governs various sports.

Big Ten Conference meet A track meet held toward the end of the season with the top participants from schools in the Big Ten Conference.

dictator A ruler with absolute, unrestricted power.

discrimination A difference in treatment or consideration of a group of people based on the group, class, or category to which a person belongs rather than based on merit.

exhibition A public display of athletic skill that is not an official competition.

foul In the long jump, an attempt that is not counted due to the athlete overstepping the end of the takeoff board prior to leaving his or her feet.

Great Black Migration The relocation of more than six million African Americans from the rural South to the cities of the North, Midwest, and West from 1916 to 1970.

hit the tape Slang for crossing the finish line in first place.

integrated A place or an institution where people from different ethnic or racial backgrounds are brought together.

long jump A jump for distance from a running start.

Olympic trials A competition among top athletes to determine who will represent their country in the Olympic Games.

pit The sand into which long jumpers jump.

prejudice An unfavorable opinion or feeling about a group of people formed without knowledge, thought, or sufficient reason.

relay A race between two or more teams of contestants, each contestant being relieved by a teammate after running part of the distance. In track and field, there are usually four competitors on each team running the same distance.

run through A practice routine often done by long jumpers to gauge their foot patterns; not meant to be counted as a jump attempt.

GLOSSARY

segregation The separation of people of different ethnic groups in housing, work, or education.

stance The position of the body while standing or prior to competing.

starting blocks A device used by runners, especially sprinters, for increasing their speed at the beginning of a race; usually consists of a metal or wooden frame secured to the ground at both ends. When tracks were natural surfaces topped with cinders, runners dug their own footholds in the track.

stride The distance covered by one step.

United States Olympic Committee The organization charged with supporting, entering, and overseeing teams and individuals representing the United States in the Olympic Games. During Jesse Owens's time, it was known as the American Olympic Association.

SELECTED BIBLIOGRAPHY

Books

Baker, William J. *Jesse Owens: An American Life*. New York: The Free Press, 1986.

Burlingame, Jeff. *Jesse Owens: "I Always Loved Running."* Berkeley Heights, NJ: Enslow Publishers, Inc., 2011.

Gentry, Tony. *Jesse Owens: Champion Athlete*. Philadelphia: Chelsea House Publishers, 2005.

Josephson, Judith Pinkerton. *Jesse Owens: Track and Field Legend*. Springfield, IL: Enslow Publishers, Inc., 1997.

McKissack, Patricia, and Fredrick McKissack. *Jesse Owens: Olympic Star.* Hillside, NJ: Enslow Publishers, Inc., 1992.

Streissguth, Tom. *Jesse Owens.* Minneapolis: Lerner Publications Company, 1999.

Online Articles

Anderson, Dave. "Carl Lewis Once Met Jesse Owens." *Star-News*. July 23, 1984. news.google.com/newspapers?nid=1454&dat=19840723&id=GFhOAAAAIBAJ&sjid=pBMEAAAAIBAJ&pg=5975,6474735&hl=en.

Dyer, Kristian. "Inspirational Moments: Carl Lewis' meeting with Jesse Owens." *Yahoo Sports*. July 26, 2012. sports.yahoo.com/blogs/fourth-place-medal/

inspirational-moments-carl-lewis-meeting-jesse-owens-132112251--oly.html.

"From the Vault: Jesse Owens In His Own Words." March 31, 2008. *The Guardian.* www.theguardian.com/sport/blog/2008/apr/01/fromthevaultjesseowensin.

Haire, Kevlin. "Jesse Owens: A Lasting Legend." *The Ohio State University Archives.* 2010. library.osu.edu/projects/jesse-owens/timeline.html.

"Jesse Owens – Related Biography: Coach Charles Riley." sports.jrank.org/pages/3576/Owens-Jesse-Related-Biography-Coach-Charles-Riley.html.

"Jewish Athletes: Marty Glickman & Sam Stoller." *United States Holocaust Memorial Museum*. www.ushmm.org/exhibition/olympics/?content=jewish_athletes_more&lang=en.

Schwartz, Larry. "An American Hero." *ESPN SportsCentury.* espn.go.com/sportscentury/features/00194717.html.

———. "Owens Pierced a Myth." *ESPN SportsCentury.* espn.go.com/sportscentury/features/00016393.html.

FURTHER INFORMATION

Books

Nuwer, Hank. *The Legend of Jesse Owens*. New York: Franklin Watts, 1998.

Owens, Jesse, and Paul G. Neimark. *The Jesse Owens Story.* New York: G. P. Putnam's Sons, 1970.

Schaap, Jeremy. *Triumph: The Untold Story of Jesse Owens and Hitler's Olympics*. Boston: Houghton Mifflin Company, 2007.

Videos

Jesse Owens 1936 Olympics Highlights
www.youtube.com/watch?v=HCmvDwDocrw

This video captures Jesse Owens competing in the 1936 Olympic Games with clips of Adolf Hitler's reaction to Owens's victories.

Jesse Owens: Enduring Spirit
www.youtube.com/watch?v=gn-Xg158TcQ

This twenty-eight-minute documentary chronicles the life, trials, and triumphs of Jesse Owens, produced by WOSU Public Media, out of Ohio.

Jesse Owens vs. Hitler
www.history.com/videos/jesse-owens-vs-hitler#jesse-owens-vs-hitler

Comedian Michael Loftus offers a humorous perspective on Jesse Owens's success in the 1936 Olympics.

FURTHER INFORMATION

PBS American Experience & Jesse Owens

www.youtube.com/watch?v=8pUXMHr_pao

View this fifty-five-minute documentary on Jesse Owens produced by PBS.

Organizations

Jesse Owens Foundation

www.jesse-owens.org/about1.html

Jesse Owens Website

JesseOwens.com

Olympic Movement Jesse Owens Biography

Olympic.org/jesse-owens

INDEX

Page numbers in **boldface** are illustrations. Entries in **boldface** are glossary terms.

1936 Olympics, 4–5, 19, 39–40, 47, 49, 52, 75, 86
  400-meter relay controversy, 62–65, 68–69
  new technology, 52–53
  possible boycott, 42
Amateur Athletic Union (AAU), 30, 38–41, 44, 71, 74, 78, 81
Aryan, 4, 41, 50–51, 53, 58, 60

Beamon, Bob, **93**
Big Ten, 5, 45–46
Big Ten Conference meet/championships, 30, 34, **36–37**
Blackthink, 61, 90
Brundage, Avery, 42, **43**, 66–67, 74

dictator, 4, 44, 49, 51–52
discrimination, 5, 27, 43, 45, 52, 68, 90, 101

equal rights, 4
exhibition, 30, 71–72, 74, 81, 83, 86

foul, 58–60

Glickman, Marty, 65–68, **67**
Great Black Migration, 12

hit the tape, 19
Hitler, Adolf, 4–5, 39, 41–42, 44, **48**, 49–56, **54**, 59–61, 64, 67, 69, 96

integrated, 25
International Olympic Committee, 39, 41, 55
Jesse Owens Story, The, 10, 13, 16, 26, 29, 34, 49, 51, 60, 71, 100

Legend of Jesse Owens, The, 15–16, 22, 26, 32, 41, 96

INDEX

Long, Carl Ludwig "Luz," **57**, 58–61, **59**

long jump, 5, 16, 22–23, 25, 29–30, 34, 40, 46, 58–59, 66, 72, 85–86, 94

Louis, Joe, 47, 78, 92, 96

Metcalfe, Ralph, 22–23, **24**, 30, 34–35, 54, **62**, 65, 68–69

Nazi party, 39, 41–43, 49, 51, 54, 67

National Collegiate Athletic Association (NCAA), 27, 40, 92

Ohio State University, 26–27, **28**, 30–31, 35, 40, 45, 53, 66, 68, 83, 86–87, 92, 97

Olympic trials, 22, 42, 46

Owens, Jesse, **6–8**, **11**, **14**, **21**, **24**, **28**, **36–37**, **46**, **57**, **59**, **62**, **70**, **73**, **76–77**, **82**, **84**, **91**, **93**

- early life, 9–12
- early education, 11, 17
- father, 9–10, **11**, 12–13
- marriage, 20, **21**, 38
- mother, 10, **11**, 12–13, 16, 18, 20
- post-Olympic careers, 75, 81, 83–85
- records and awards, 40, 86–87, 92, 97

Owens, Ruth Solomon, **11**, 20, **21**, 22–23, 38, **79**, **95**

Paddock, Charley, 17, 38

Peacock, Eulace, 38, 45, **46**

pit, 34, 58–59, 94

prejudice, 4, 12, 26, 44, 60

racism, 32, 42, 89–90

relay, 5, 17, 30, 40, **62–63**, 64–68, 72–74, 94

Riley, Charles, 4, 13, 15–19, 22, 25–26, 35, 78, 86

Roosevelt, Franklin D., 5, 75

run through, 58

segregation, 18, 33, **33**
Snyder, Larry, 28, 29–30, 33–35, 43–44, 53, 68, 72–74
stance (in track and field), 29, 32
stride, 58
starting blocks, 35, 45, 55

United States Olympic Committee, the, 67

World War II, 60, 67, 69, 83

ABOUT THE AUTHOR

Jackie F. Stanmyre is a former award-winning journalist at the *Star-Ledger* of Newark, New Jersey, where she wrote enterprise stories on issues surrounding athletics in addition to extensive profiles about interesting personalities in sports. She currently works as a mental health and addiction counselor. She lives in Montclair, New Jersey, with her husband and son and their two cats.